**FAN
PHENOMENA**

TWIN
PEAKS

**EDITED BY
MARISA C. HAYES
AND FRANCK BOULÈGUE**

Credits

First Published in the UK in 2013 by Intellect Books,
The Mill, Parnall Road, Fishponds, Bristol, BS16 3JG, UK

First Published in the USA in 2013 by Intellect Books,
The University of Chicago Press, 1427 E. 60th Street,
Chicago, IL 60637, USA

Editors: Marisa C. Hayes and Franck Boulègue

Series Editor and Design: Gabriel Solomons

Copy Editor: Michael Eckhardt

A Catalogue record for this book is available from
the British Library

Fan Phenomena Series
ISSN: 2051-4468
eISSN: 2051-4476

Fan Phenomena: Twin Peaks
ISBN: 978-1-78320-024-5
eISBN: 978-1-78320-102-0 / 978-1-78320-101-3

Printed and bound by
Bell & Bain Limited, Glasgow

Contents

Acknowledgements

First generation fans of *Twin Peaks* often relate to experiences of sneaking out of bed to catch a glimpse of the show when it first aired, arguing with family members who insisted on changing the channel when the man from another place began to dance, or daring to voice admiration for the feature film that was universally rejected by critics when first released. Newer fans probably didn't have to struggle as much to defend their love of *Twin Peaks*, but they continue to breathe new life and creativity into its thriving community. To fans of all generations, this book is first and foremost for you.

It would be impossible to continue without first thanking the two figures whose imagination, courage, and artistry brought *Twin Peaks* to the world, David Lynch and Mark Frost. Their stories and images have touched many of us, aided by additional collaborators whose music, writing, and support were instrumental in shaping the Twin Peaks universe, particularly: Angelo Badalamenti, Jennifer Chambers Lynch, Scott Frost, and Michel Chion. We also extend our thanks to the cast and crew of *Twin Peaks*, an unforgettable ensemble of talented actors and technicians who created magic for both the small and big screen.

Our deep appreciation goes out to this book's wonderful group of contributors. Their essays tackle a diverse and fascinating set of subjects that illustrate a deep love for *Twin Peaks* alongside innovative ways of approaching and understanding the series and film. We also wish to thank Intellect for their vision in creating the *Fan Pheomena* book series under the leadership of Gabriel Solomons, series editor. We are particularly grateful for his support and assistance in developing the book with us, and for having accepted our proposal to add a *Twin Peaks* title to the collection. We also thank the artists and interview subjects of this book who gave their time and passion so willingly to this collective project.

See you in our dreams....

Marisa C. Hayes & Franck Boulègue

Introduction
Marisa C. Hayes, with Franck Boulègue, co-editors

→ Welcome to Twin Peaks! The sign of this mythic town reads 'population 51,201', but its impact is far greater than the number implies. More than 20 years have passed since David Lynch and Mark Frost's groundbreaking series first debuted on ABC, but the demand for *Twin Peaks*-inspired scholarship, events, screenings and merchandise has only continued to grow worldwide. Like many great works of art, *Twin Peaks* was ahead of its time and multi-layered, resulting in a show and feature film that remain fresh and evocative today.

Fig. 1: The Twin Peaks town mayor initiating in the pilot episode.

We are thrilled that *Twin Peaks* is the subject of this volume in Intellect's new *Fan Phenomena* series. These books are dedicated to providing an entertaining and informative look at cultural icons, and their ongoing impact in the areas of fan media, philosophy, economy, fashion, language and more. The process of co-editing this book has convinced us more than ever of *Twin Peaks'* rightful place in the *Fan Phenomena* series. Not only did our call for papers elicit an impressive number of compelling and intriguing essays from long-time fans and scholars (enough to fill multiple volumes), but as the book advanced, so did our knowledge of *Twin Peaks* aficionados and events around the world. From recent screenings of *Twin Peaks: Fire Walk with Me* (Lynch, 1992) at the National Museum of Singapore to Portland, Oregon's 'Black Lodge Burlesque' performances at the historic Star Theatre, *Twin Peaks* continues to manifest and reinvent itself in the post-broadcast era.

When it first aired in 1990, audiences responded favourably to *Twin Peaks'* pilot episode (dir. David Lynch), appreciative of the show's genre-bending 'whodunnit' and quirky characters. The shaky reception following the series' surreal third episode (dir. David Lynch), however, marked a decline in viewing numbers. Other conflicts, including network pressure to reveal Laura Palmer's murderer in the second season, sealed the deal. It's a wonder that the show's final episodes even aired at all, the direct result of a successful letter writing campaign initiated by fans (one of the many *Twin Peaks* precedents that shaped contemporary TV culture). *Twin Peaks* was cancelled after only two short seasons and a total of 30 episodes. At first glance, such numbers don't instil a sense of just how influential *Twin Peaks* was and continues to be – but what is in a number?

When we refer to a show's impact within the realm of fan phenomena, we move far beyond the game of numbers that determines the initial airtime of any given series. The shows and films that persevere do so because they strike a chord within a dedicated, passionate group of followers. Such programmes are often rejected by mainstream audiences or studios for being too 'inaccessible', 'offbeat' or 'controversial', as witnessed

Introduction
Marisa C. Hayes, with Franck Boulègue, co-editors

with *Twin Peaks*. The show's vibrant and richly layered dream sequences, for instance, resemble what general audiences might stereotypically expect to find at a video art exhibition, not on network television. Yet, it is often these very elements that are credited with building and extending a show or film's lasting cult following.

Many of the viewers who abandoned *Twin Peaks* midway through its initial broadcast exclaimed, 'I have no idea what's going on' or, 'This is weird!' uncomfortable with the unexplained. As David Lynch recently quipped in the programme notes for his latest film *Inland Empire (2006):* 'I don't know why people expect art to make sense when they accept the fact that life doesn't make sense.' Fortunately, *Twin Peaks'* entire run continued to resonate with a loyal group of fans; viewers who are patient enough to digest the show's symbolism in their own way, embracing both the light-hearted and comedic aspects of *Twin Peaks* alongside its significant look at the darker side of human nature. The same can be said for Lynch's French-backed feature film, *Twin Peaks: Fire Walk with Me*. While its release was considered a commercial failure in North America and was even booed by audiences at the Cannes Film Festival, the movie has undergone critical re-evaluation in recent years, with some film scholars declaring it a 'masterpiece'. Certainly, some fans of the series are divided on the subject, but *Twin Peaks: Fire Walk with Me* continues to elicit a cult-like appreciation as special edition DVD sales and film journals will confirm. In this volume, some contributors have chosen to focus exclusively on either the series or the film, while others freely reference both. Whether you have a preference for one or the other, the symbiotic relationship of the *Twin Peaks* film and series is undeniable. To truly take up residence in the town of Twin Peaks, a familiarity with both is essential.

This volume opens with an in depth look at *Twin Peaks'* profound impact on television and new media. The show's visual aesthetics, themes and artful use of music, among others, would forevermore change the nature of television, breaking barriers and paving the way for today's 'New Golden Age' of TV drama. Other essays linked to media and *Twin Peaks'* vast influence include a section that tackles Lynch's feature film *Twin Peaks: Fire Walk with Me*, and an essay examining *Twin Peaks*-inspired performance art, advertising and video. Philosophical explorations ranging from dream psychology to third-wave feminism enhance our understanding of the construction and impact of the *Twin Peaks* universe, followed by character studies that provide intimate portraits of a few of *Twin Peaks'* most beloved (or villainous) residents. These sections consider aspects of mythology or philosophy that shape our understanding of select characters' underlying nature and narrative function. Readers will observe some overlap between many of the subject areas addressed within these pages, which only attests further to the rich and complex web that is *Twin Peaks*, a phenomenon incapable of being categorized neatly in any one box. Audrey Horne, for example, is the focus of a fashion essay, which also serves as a clever character analysis. Another section on *Twin Peaks* memorabilia provides additional knowledge in the fields of economics and fashion, while a section that explores the topography of *Twin Peaks* creates an interdisciplinary character study of the town itself, merging aspects of sound, language and philosophy.

From these insightful and accessible essays, readers will easily observe that the *Twin Peaks* universe continues to assert its lasting impact, transcending the barriers of time and place. Those hungry for more information shouldn't forget to consult the book's 'Going Further' section, a list of the best *Twin Peaks* resources handpicked by our contributors. We hope you'll enjoy exploring the infinite wonder of *Twin Peaks*, a town still filled with secrets, as a new generation of international fans will attest, alongside seasoned veterans of the show and film. So, grab a slice of cherry pie and enjoy the damn fine reading in *Fan Phenomena: Twin Peaks*! ●

Chapter
1

Peaks and
Pop Culture

Shara Lorea Clark

→ 'Who killed Laura Palmer?' In 1990, this chilling question drew unsuspecting audiences to ABC to follow quirky FBI Special Agent Dale Cooper in his mission to solve the mysterious murder of a high school homecoming queen. On the night of its premier, 34.6 million viewers tuned in for the feature-length pilot (Season 1 Episode 1), and the macabre image of Laura Palmer's body found washed ashore, wrapped in plastic, became an instant icon. In a time when more auspicious sitcoms like *Cheers* (1982-93) and *Roseanne* (1988-97) topped the prime time charts, virgin audiences were introduced to something different - something way weirder than they were used to.

By way of *Twin Peaks*, David Lynch and Mark Frost brought a cinematic element of dark intrigue, unease and mystery to the screen that television audiences had not been exposed to. It was that mystery, along with the ominous woods and the somehow off-kilter picture-perfect town that enthralled a slew of fans. The transcendental Red Room scenes with the backwards-talking and dancing dwarf swept viewers off of their couches and into *Twin Peaks*' alternate universe. From there began the journey to a place both wonderful and strange. Fans became fixated on the show's wondrous world of evolving secrets, questionable owls and ever-curious overacting. Despite being intentionally offbeat, *Twin Peaks* became a worldwide sensation, ranking among the top-rated TV series of the '90s. The show's supernatural undertones, oddball characters and interdimensional dream sequences spawned a dedicated cult following and changed television in a big way. It inspired and shaped its own cult movements, as well as a series of others, that followed in its wake.

Twin Peaks' influence on popular culture reveals itself in television shows, movies, songs and other forms of media from the '90s to now. It saturated the cultural consciousness in such an immense and immediate way that not just television audiences, but also accomplished writers and directors took notice. As people obsessed over finding clues that would lead to Laura Palmer's killer, *Peaks* references began appearing in popular network shows. In 1990, before the killer was revealed, an episode of *Saturday Night Live* featured an unusually long, nine-minute parody sketch of the surreal soap. Kyle MacLachlan hosted the episode and played Agent Cooper in the skit, in which he exaggerated, if not by much, his idiosyncrasies, announcing to his tape recorder, 'Diane...this morning I showered for nine minutes, found seventeen hairs. Three curly, fourteen straight.' And a *Peaks* red herring, Leo Johnson, portrayed by Chris Farley in the skit, adamantly confessed to the crime, and showed incriminating photos of himself committing the act, but Cooper just wouldn't have it. He wanted to look deeper, continue the mystery, as the show itself did, long after the murder was solved.

Another of the first, but perhaps one of the most unusual, shows to reference *Twin Peaks* was *Sesame Street* (1969-), a popular children's television show, which spoofed the series in February 1991 during *Peaks*' second season. In the borderline creepy 'Monsterpiece Theater: Twin Beaks' segment, Cookie Monster plays Agent Cookie, an inquisitive creature who carries a tape recorder he refers to as Diane. He questions Twin Beaks residents in the diner, which of course serves 'darn fine' pie, and asks the double-beaked birds David Finch, Laura and the Log Bird about how the town got its name. They wouldn't divulge the secret.

Even the long running animated sitcom *The Simpsons* (1989-) referenced *Twin Peaks* on more than one occasion. In the 1995 episode 'Who Shot Mr. Burns Part II' (Season 7, Episode 1), Chief Wiggum dreams he is in a red-curtained room with chevron

Peaks and Pop Culture
Shara Lorea Clark

*Fig. 2: Chief Wiggum and Lisa
Simpson in a Twin Peaks-inspired
episode of The Simpsons (1989–).*

floors. Lisa dances and speaks backwards as she delivers a
clue, in the same way *Peaks'* Man from Another Place does
in Cooper's dream. Again, in the 1997 episode 'Lisa's Sax'
(Season 9, Episode 3), Homer is seen intently watching an
episode of *Twin Peaks*, in which a giant dances with a white
horse in the woods. Both a giant and a white horse played
part in *Peaks'* perplexity. Homer reacts in a manner shared with many *Peaks'* viewers by
saying, 'Brilliant! I have absolutely no idea what's going on.'

Though short-lived, airing its two seasons in just over a year, *Twin Peaks* essentially
redefined the boundaries of network television, and opened the door for many of today's well-known serial dramas and science fiction TV shows. If not for *Twin Peaks* blur-
ring the lines of what was too weird or too grotesquely odd, there may have never been
shows like *Lost* (2004–10), *Fringe* (2008–) or *American Horror Story* (2011–). And audiences almost certainly never would have seen Chris Carter's *The X-Files* (1993–2002),
arguably the first and most propitious in this list of series influenced by *Peaks*. Premier-
ing in 1993, about a year after the release of the film *Twin Peaks: Fire Walk With Me*
(Lynch, 1992), *The X-Files* followed on the heels of *Peaks'* surprising but fleeting network success.

By some accounts, *Peaks'* untimely demise came at the hands of network execu-
tives, who shuffled its time slot and insisted that the writers reveal what Lynch later
referred to as the show's 'golden egg'. Lynch has said in several interviews that by revealing Laura's killer – the show's biggest and most precious mystery – much earlier
than planned, they 'killed the goose'. After the secret was out, the show meandered into
muddled subplots, and its ratings declined. Following this experiment with *Peaks*, major networks had a newfound openness to envelope-pushing, genre-based series, and a
better understanding of how to make them work.

Perhaps as a better effort to keep audiences coming back, much of *The X-Files'*
story and background was presented via stand-alone 'monster of the week' episodes,
but there were a few 'golden eggs' that were maintained throughout the series' nine
seasons: the mystery of Agent Mulder's younger sister's abduction, for example, and the
identity of the Smoking Man were part of the show's overarching, continuous mystery.
Where *Peaks* ultimately became something of a test series, *X-Files* was able to easily
and successfully follow suit – fearlessly delving into paranormal territory while exploring conspiracy theories and government mistrust, and aiming to prove extraterrestrial
existence. Post-*Peaks* audiences were ready for it. By leaving us with some of the most
disturbing images TV viewers had seen to date, Lynch created a place for this type of
bizarre and unusual programming.

Interestingly, *The X-Files* cast also included several *Twin Peaks* mainstays. Most notably, David Duchovny, who played a cross-dressing FBI agent in *Peaks*, became the
lead male (and one half of the main duo) in *The X-Files*, playing FBI Special Agent Fox

Mulder. Agent Mulder, like *Peaks*' Cooper, exhibited an unconventional methodology and showed a deep-rooted respect for and awe of the paranormal. Don Davis, who portrayed *Peaks*' Major Briggs, appeared in the *The X-Files* as Captain William Scully, Special Agent Dana Scully's father. Other crossover actors included Richard Beymer (*Peaks*' Benjamin Horne), Kenneth Welsh (Windom Earle), Michael J. Anderson (The Man from Another Place), Michael Horse (Deputy Hawk), Jan D'Arcy (Sylvia Horne) and Frances Bay (Mrs. Tremond).

As *Peaks*' memorable one-liners – 'The owls are not what they seem' and 'Who killed Laura Palmer?' – were on the lips of anyone and everyone watching TV in the early '90s, *Files*' slogans became as omnipresent. 'The Truth is Out There', 'Trust No One', and 'I Want to Believe' became benchmarks of their time. The show went on to gain a major cult following of its own, and is known as another defining series of the '90s.

The X-Files isn't the only show that has *Twin Peaks* to thank for setting new standards for what was previously banally formulaic television. Fast-forward to 2004, when audiences were introduced to *Lost*, a strange and enigmatic show from creators Jeffrey Lieber, J.J. Abrams and Damon Lindelof. In an interview with CHUD.com's Devin Faraci, Lindelof said he and his father watched *Twin Peaks* every week when it originally aired: 'He'd tape the show on his VCR, and we'd watch the episode again right after it aired in our quest to pull every last clue out of the show,' Lindelof said. 'The idea of a TV show being a mystery and a game that spawned hundreds of theories obviously was a major precedent – that's a fancy way of saying we ripped it off – for *Lost*.'

Lindelof's admission aside, *Peaks*' influences are more than obvious in *Lost*, which in many ways was something of a next generation *Twin Peaks*. *Lost* left viewers on the edge of their seats, anxiously awaiting clues and answers. What's up with that smoke monster? What happens if they don't push the button? These and other questions had fans wildly obsessing over the island's mystique. In the bigger picture, *Lost* played heavily on duality, much like *Twin Peaks*. The juxtaposition of black-and-white is a recurring motif, representing moral and spiritual dualism in the show's characters and their various conflicts. The discordance between the passengers of Oceanic Airlines Flight 815 and the island's seemingly malicious inhabitants known as 'The Others' reiterates the show's dualistic nature.

With its puzzling subplots and clues that many times led nowhere, *Lost* embraced what *Twin Peaks* had set out to do by presenting viewers with a slowly unraveling mystery in a strange setting. It presented a hard code to crack, and, like *Peaks*, left viewers with a somewhat open-ended conclusion that left plenty of room for theories and unending discussion. *Lost* created a hubbub bigger than just about any other show in the 2000s, and has been praised by many critics as one of the best TV serials of all time.

Lost co-creator Abrams, who has had a hand in creating a plethora of sci-fi and paranormal TV shows and movies, further proves the influence of *Twin Peaks* on his work in other projects. The newer FOX sci-fi drama *Fringe*, for example, which is very much

Peaks and Pop Culture
Shara Lorea Clark

Fig. 3: FOX's Fringe references Dr. Jacoby of Twin Peaks in the episode Northwest Passage (2010).

like *The X-Files*, also delves into parallel universes where the characters' alternate selves reside. *Fringe* writers have made notable references to *Twin Peaks*, several in the episode 'Northwest Passage' (Season 2, Episode 21), which shares a title with the *Twin Peaks* pilot, and was also the originally-intended name of the series itself. In the episode, Walter is seen wearing a pair of red and blue-lensed glasses that allow him to see his patient's aura. He mentions that his friend Dr. Jacoby from Washington state invented the spectacles. They are the same style of coloured-lens eyeglasses that *Peaks'* eccentric psychiatrist Dr. Lawrence Jacoby famously wore.

In 2010, the year of *Twin Peaks'* 20th anniversary, several tributes were made in recognition of this milestone. A nod was given by voice actor and rapper MC Chris in the form of a special April Fool's Day song uploaded to his website. The eponymous song starts:

Stack up the donuts; pack up the pies.
Put on the trench coat; rack up the lies [...]
Gotta crack a case in a place called Peaks;
Where the lights all blink and your outlook's bleak.
Got a lotta caffeine;
Interrogating teens 'cause the homecoming queen just rolled up on the beach,
Wrapped in plastic, white as a sheet.

An accompanying fan video made from *Twin Peaks* clips has had nearly 150,000 views on YouTube.

Another well-done anniversary tribute was a *Twin Peaks'* reunion episode of the detective comedy drama, *Psych* (2006–). Wittingly titled 'Dual Spires' (Season 5, Episode 12), the episode paid homage with even the smallest details. The show's theme music, rerecorded by *Peaks* crooner Julee Cruise, follows the opening scene, where we see private investigator Shawn sitting with his laptop pondering an article that mentioned the invention of silent window shades. The camera pans across a chocolate bunny on his desk as his partner Gus says, 'Since when is the opening and closing of shades so disruptive that it needs to be alleviated?' Within those first few seconds, they referenced *Twin Peaks'* Nadine, who prided herself on inventing silent drape runners. The bunny subtly poked at an esoteric *Peaks'* quote from Agent Cooper: 'Diane, I am holding in my hands a small box of chocolate bunnies.'

A handful of actors who played main characters in *Twin Peaks'* guest-starred in the whodunnit episode, in which a peculiar e-mail led the duo to the small town of Dual Spires and its annual cinnamon festival. They inadvertently get caught up in an investigation of the murder of high-schooler Paula Merral – an anagram of Laura Palmer.

Fig. 4: Detective drama Psych
(2006–) pays homage to Twin
Peaks in the episode Dual
Spires (2010).

Among the *Peaks* actors to appear were Sheryl Lee (*Peaks*' Laura Palmer), Sherilyn Fenn (Audrey Horne), Dana Ashbrook (Bobby Briggs), Ray Wise (Leland Palmer), Lenny Von Dohlen (Harold Smith), Robyn Lively (Lana Milford) and Catherine E. Coulson (the Log Lady). Like in *Peaks*, the victim was found shoreside wrapped in plastic, and the resulting investigation uncovered long-held secrets and sabotage. In the episode's final scene, patrons of the town's Sawmill Diner are seen dancing to sombre, swaying music and behaving strangely.

In 2011, AMC unveiled Veena Sud's *The Killing*, a murder mystery with an eerily similar plot line to *Peaks*. The first season's DVD cover art shows a close-up image of the teenage victim with the words 'Who killed Rosie Larsen?' scrawled over her face. The crime drama explores the darkest pits of human emotion, showing Rosie's parents' intense reactions after identifying their daughter's body in the morgue. The show's representation of the grieving process in such a traumatic situation is reminiscent of Leland and Sarah Palmer's heart-wrenching outbursts upon hearing the news of Laura's death in *Twin Peaks*. Though *The Killing* has shown no ties to the paranormal, its second season is set to uncover family secrets and conspiracies as *Peaks* did. And so the list of shows influenced by *Twin Peaks* grows.

Twin Peaks not only influenced what we see on our screens, but also inspired a continuously growing fanbase to create their own media and tributes. Super fans of the show continue to memorialize it by hosting viewing parties, art exhibits and fan conventions. Perhaps the most established of these is the fan-organized 'Twin Peaks Fest', held annually, near filming locations in North Bend and Snoqualmie Valley, Washington. Since its inception in 1993, the weekend-long event has drawn hundreds of diehard fans, old and new, yearly to those same ominous woods among the Douglas firs that Agent Cooper so loved.

Early ticket-buyers can snag a pass that includes a bus tour with stops at popular *Peaks*' locales like the Double R Diner (now Twede's Cafe, still serving that famous cherry pie), the Roadhouse, and the rocky shore where Laura's body was found. The fest's agenda also includes *Twin Peaks* costume and trivia contests, Tibetan rock-throwing and cherry stem-tying contests, movie night, and a bounty of doughnuts and damn fine

Peaks and Pop Culture
Shara Lorea Clark

Fig. 5: AMC's The Killing (2011–)
appropriates the Twin Peaks tagline
'Who Killed Laura Palmer?'

coffee. The main event is a celebrity dinner and Q&A, and the guest list over the years has included Sherilyn Fenn, Sheryl Lee, Ray Wise, Michael J. Anderson, Catherine E. Coulson, and many others. *Peaks* freaks are able to gain insight into some of their favourite scenes and hear stories about the actors' filming experiences. For fans, it is not only a way to get closer to their favourite otherworldly show, but also to share their love for it with others who feel the same way. Many attendees have come to treat it as a sort of family reunion and make the trek annually.

The newer 'Twin Peaks UK Festival' debuted in 2010 in conjunction with the series' 20th anniversary. Like the original Twin Peaks Fest, the event agenda includes Lynch-related screenings and of course lots of doughnuts, cherry pie and David Lynch-brand coffee. Attendees also delight in *Peaks*-fuelled burlesque and cabaret performances. In 2010, Julee Cruise stopped by to perform some of the famously ethereal soundtrack songs like 'Falling' and 'Into the Night'. Other *Peaks* actors who have attended the event include Kimmy Robertson (Lucy Moran), Al Strobel (the One-Armed Man), Catherine E. Coulson and Charlotte Stewart (Betty Briggs).

Beyond keeping *Twin Peaks* alive through fan conventions and gatherings, the show maintains a virtual life via fan websites, message boards and blogs. 'Welcome to Twin Peaks' – welcometotwinpeaks.com – for example, features updates on everything *Twin Peaks*. The site claims to be 'filling the donut hole in your post-*Peaks* life.' Its 'freshly squeezed posts' provide info on the cast members' current projects and public appearances, as well as details on *Peaks* and Lynch events worldwide. An 'inspiration' tab on the site is dedicated to fan art and media, and the site's shop offers T-shirts, books, posters and other *Peaks* treasures. The site's Facebook page currently boasts nearly 4000 fans, and each 'like' brings them 'closer to a population of 51,201' – their goal, the population of *Twin Peaks*.

Several other *Twin Peaks* fan blogs and sites exist, and fan Jak Locke has even created an Atari-style video game, 'Black Lodge 2600', which is available as a free download for PC and Mac. The gamer's goal is to escape the Black Lodge while avoiding obstacles and running from pesky doppelgängers.

Luckily for *Twin Peaks* fans, the waves it has made pop culturally have yet to subside, and if the evidence of its continuing influence is any indication, its impact will be seen for years to come. Now that the entire series is available on DVD and has recently been added to Netflix's instant streaming offerings, more and more people are being turned on to its unapologetically wacky world. Now more than ever, fan fodder abounds. Whether presented through our TV or computer screens, at art exhibits or fan festivals, its tale continues to unfold. By keeping up with its virtual presence and continuing to gather to revel in its existence, fans can hold on to the dream that maybe on some other

Fig. 6: Jak Locke's Atari-style video game, Black Lodge 2600.

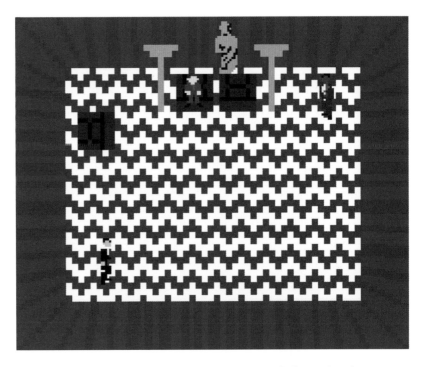

Fig. 6: Jak Locke's Atari-style video game, Black Lodge 2600.

Lynchian plane, the *Twin Peaks* universe remains very much alive, and its characters are still dreamily jazz-dancing to Angelo Badalamenti tunes in the mysteriously quirky small town that forever changed the world. ●

Fan Appreciation no.1
Bryan Hogue: Co-owner 'Black Lodge Video'

Interview by Shara Lorea Clark

'..A place of almost unimaginable power...a power so vast that its bearer might reorder the Earth itself to his liking...This place I speak of is known as the Black Lodge – and I intend to find it.' - Windom Earle

A Black Lodge has been found in Memphis, Tennessee. Though Deputy Hawk warned those passing through the Lodge to do so with perfect courage lest their souls be annihilated, people have passed through this Lodge for over a decade, souls still intact.

Opened in 2000 by *Peaks* fans Bryan Hogue and Matthew Martin, Black Lodge Video is a Memphis gem. The rental store's on-street sign shows Agent Cooper peeking through red curtains, and its shelves feature a selection of thousands of obscure and classic movies in all formats, including many VHS. The films are organized by directors, countries, themes and genres, and there's a permanent space for David Lynch's work.

Shara Lorea Clark: How did your first *Peaks* experience affect you?
Bryan Hogue: My first exposure to it was strange. I caught one episode midway through season two – the one where the horse appeared in the living room. It made no sense. When the whole series was released, I watched it all in one run. For that day and a half, I existed in *Twin Peaks*. It was a heavy, concentrated experience. The ending is so crushing and cool and heartbreaking. From there, I became pretty obsessed with it. Matt, my business partner, was into it too, which was one of the things we connected on.

SLC: How did this fascination with *Peaks* translate into naming the store Black Lodge Video?
BH: Matt and I collected VHS and had built up a healthy collection. When we decided to open a store, we knew the name had to be something that meant a lot to us. We were *Peaks* freaks for years and wanted to give it props.

SLC: The Lodge is on Cooper Street. Coincidence?
BH: After we chose the location, a week passed before I thought, '831 South Cooper...Black Lodge Video...holy shit!' It's at Cooper and Evelyn. Evelyn was the woman James Hurley visited. Also, the place across the street, that's Palmer Real Estate. We've got all kinds of little *Twin Peaks* nods around us, but it was complete coincidence.

'Fellas, coincidence and fate figure largely in our lives.' - Agent Cooper

Fan Appreciation no.1

SLC: Who is your favorite *Twin Peaks* character and why?
BH: The obvious answer would be Cooper. But Major Briggs, brilliantly played by the late Don Davis, is such a complex and warm character that you can't help but love every second he's on screen. He was a unique pillar of confidence and strength, but then there are times where his deadpan, introverted persona is turned inside out by moments of tenderness. Who doesn't love the scene in the diner where he tells his son, Bobby, about the dream he had about them? Time stops for me every time I see it. Or even Briggs' truth serum response to Windom Earle's question: "What do you fear most in the world?" Briggs: "The possibility that love is not enough." That's one of the most beautiful and naive notions I've ever heard; a philosophy few wouldn't be crushed by the weight of. I always felt that Briggs' depth and spiritual scope probably surpassed even Coops.

SLC: What are your feelings about the series versus the movie?
BH: I know it's going to sound blasphemous, but I think the movie ended up being a wasted opportunity for either closure to our storyline or at least taking it a few steps further than the end of the series. I never thought the movie added anything new to the overall story. In the series, we got plenty of information about Laura, her double life, and troubles as the mystery unfolded. Did we really need a whole movie devoted to seeing it? I've watched it several times, and it does have its good moments. It just always makes me wish for what could have been. There have been rumors about the massive amount that was cut from *Fire Walk With Me*. Maybe one day Frost and Lynch will be able to and want to restore it to what they originally envisioned.

SLC: Why do you think the series/film has weathered the test of time?
BH: I guess it stands as a testament to not always treating your audience

like idiots and going for what feels right; no matter how against the grain it might be. I like to believe Lynch's influence is as much to thank for that as anything else. I think the mystery of Laura's murder is what interested most at first. Then once you delve into all of the other characters in the town and the mechanics of their lives, that's when you realize how densely layered their world is. Once its dark tone starts to show, either it turned you off or made you crave more. And many of us craved more. It's just an amazingly well constructed mindf**k, and my world is richer for having been exposed to it.

SLC: How would you describe *Peaks'* influence on pop culture/television?
BH: *Peaks* opened up a cerebral side in TV, challenging viewers to look beneath the surface of its whodunit narrative and to process the deeper chemistry of its characters and their world. It exposed layers of secrets, lies, fears, desires, spirituality and inevitable doom. *Peaks* showed us that good does not always conquer evil, and that even the strong and pure are vulnerable. The giant in *Peaks* said that "a path is formed by laying one stone at a time." *Twin Peaks*, I believe, is that first stone on the path to smarter television. It did what few shows did before it or since – it turned television into art. ●

———

Fig. 2 (opposite): Co-owner Matthew Martin with Grace Zabriskie (Sarah Palmer)

———

Fig. 3 (opposite) A Black Lodge tribute photo taken for the Welcome to Twin Peaks photo project (Shara Lorea Klark

Chapter
2

Audrey in Five Outfits

Angela K. Bayout

→ Browsing racks of clothing at San Francisco's vintage boutique Held Over, I noticed familiar music playing in the air. It sounded like something from *Blue Velvet* (Lynch, 1986) – something very David Lynch. I thought that was funny because I actually had the first DVD of *Twin Peaks* (1990–91) waiting for me at home, and I planned on watching it that night.

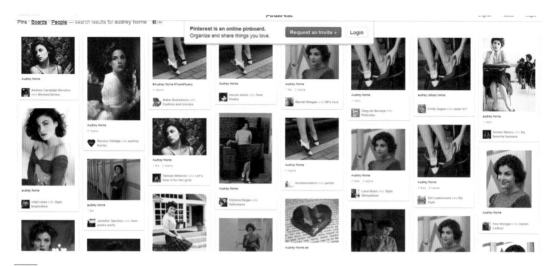

Fig. 1:
Audrey on Pinterest.com.

'No,' I said aloud, 'this is actually the *Twin Peaks* soundtrack.' I eventually recognized that echoing baritone guitar from when the series first aired and I was seven or eight. At that moment in the shop, I didn't yet know that a month later I would be back at this store and online seeking clothes just like the ones Audrey Horne wears. Thinking back, this was the kind of serendipity Gordon Cole's team of FBI agents would encounter.

The two black pencil skirts, forest-green sweater, retro cashmere top, three vintage cardigans and pair of saddle shoes that I ended up buying over the course of my *Twin Peaks* rediscovery in December 2010, represent the infatuation that I, and many others all over the Internet, have with Audrey.

Sherilyn Fenn's notorious character became a television sex symbol while *Twin Peaks* first ran. Her style is an anachronism, but she wears grandma's old clothing oh-so-well. While her attractiveness is undeniable, Audrey isn't just a young, pretty girl. She's as complicated as Pete's multi-layered flannel fishing outfit. As Fenn acknowledged at a May 2012 convention, '[Audrey] stood the test of time.' Since February 2011, when the series became available on Netflix Instant, Audrey's depth of character has been redis-covered and appreciated by a whole new generation of young women using the Internet as their megaphone. Audrey Horne is a heroine to these individuals, and officially a style icon.

Do a web search for 'Audrey Horne style', and you'll find numerous sites and links featuring her wardrobe. The short but piquant brunette has a look that's being shared via virtually-curated outfits on social shopping sites like Polyvore and Kaboodle, via .gif and

Audrey in Five Outfits
Angela K. Bayout

Fig. 2: A recent Audrey-inspired collage on Etsy (http://www.etsy.com/blog/en/2011/visit-twin-peaks-with-honey-kennedy/).

image sharing sites like Tumblr and Pinterest, and via independent blogs. These platforms allow fans to indulge in the show's rich and quirky visuals in a way that didn't exist during the early '90s, especially when it comes to Audrey's deceptively simple look. Pairing '50s plaid skirts, fitted sweaters and striking brogues with her voluptuous bob and twinkling eyes, Audrey wears an ensemble that dazzles web savvy fashion aficionados and vintage lovers. Patricia Norris, who won an Emmy for costuming the pilot, actually sourced second-hand and vintage material from thrift shops, according to a 1990 *Seattle Times* article. Many of the looks from the show's start are authentic.

The audience, picking up on the fashion appeal of *Twin Peaks*,like me, often shops independent e-retailers. Etsy, the top online site for vintage, has thousands of plaid

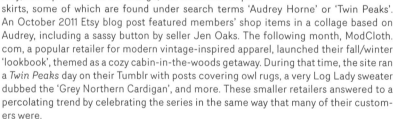

skirts, some of which are found under search terms 'Audrey Horne' or 'Twin Peaks'. An October 2011 Etsy blog post featured members' shop items in a collage based on Audrey, including a sassy button by seller Jen Oaks. The following month, ModCloth.com, a popular retailer for modern vintage-inspired apparel, launched their fall/winter 'lookbook', themed as a cozy cabin-in-the-woods getaway. During that time, the site ran a *Twin Peaks* day on their Tumblr with posts covering owl rugs, a very Log Lady sweater dubbed the 'Grey Northern Cardigan', and more. These smaller retailers answered to a percolating trend by celebrating the series in the same way that many of their customers were.

Meanwhile, high-end designs by Chanel, Diane Von Furstenberg and Stella McCartney were styled in *W* magazine's editorial 'Sweet & Vicious'. In the spread, three sultry models pose listlessly in chiffon frocks, short-sleeved sweaters and loafers, under blue lights and in front of heavy red drapes. *W* does not explicitly state that the piece was inspired by *Twin Peaks*, but fans and non-fans alike will agree that it lives up to its Lynch-like tagline: 'Fifties glamour and a schoolgirl-meets-vixen charm set the stage for one sexy thriller.' And, while *W*'s piece was closer to couture than thrift store, it still plucked a string with those of us scouring racks at St.Vincent de Paul's for Audrey-worthy '50s woollens.

The 1950s is a poignant era to emulate in *Twin Peaks*. Mid-century Americana evokes images of wise and protective fathers pruning lawns, trusty Dalmatians riding fire trucks, and clean, white bobby socks folded crisp and neat. But like any other decade, violence and deviance drove passions and fears. Audrey's wardrobe is the innocent front of the '50s, which makes the pain of Laura's death pinch deeper than a zipper on a snug pencil skirt. On the other hand, her look pairs as perfectly with the danger of her hometown as Spanx under that pencil skirt. And it's not just what she's wearing, but how she wears it.

Fig. 3: From saddle shoes to red heels.

When you do that Internet search for Audrey's clothing, you'll most likely find her in a handful of particular outfits. There are several looks that pop up often enough to consider them significant. Here, five will be tried on and explored for how they fit into the show's story and into the life of the fashion-loving, heroine seeking audience that has made her a style icon.

A divided pair

Guaranteed you'll find this image from the pilot in any 'Audrey Horne style' web search: she's at her locker, her left foot is kicked back so that she can remove her goody-goody saddle shoe, while her right foot is already snug in a lipstick-red heel, a shoe she didn't leave home wearing. 'Audrey Horne's switch from saddle shoes to heels, moments later, is the first sign that nothing – as long as the show lasts – will ever be as it seems,' writes *Worn Fashion Magazine*'s Stephanie Fereiro. To expand on that, this shot of the black and white flat versus the red heel establishes the show's theme of duality, opposites, twin-ness, and so on. The shoes are a motif just like Laura's broken-heart necklace, the Lodges and doppelgängers.

Just a few lockers down, Donna Hayward giggles at Audrey's stashed ashtray. Donna's outfit of earthen oranges and black in a modest maxi skirt and bulky cardigan look like it came from Catherine Martell's yard sale. Numerous times throughout the series, Donna dresses like she doesn't know how to. Even though she looks very similar to Audrey, she sleuths around town in oversized down vests, and awkwardly dons Laura's old sunglasses while picking up smoking, making her much less elegant and snappy than her counterpart. Clearly, Audrey wins the proverbial walk-off at the Packard Mill.

The image may not be popular because of its thematic symbolism, but because it depicts an act that women can relate to. Sometimes it's difficult for teenage girls to express themselves through fashion around their families, especially when the fashions are tight and low-cut. At home, Audrey plays an angel in disguise, attempting to

Audrey in Five Outfits
Angela K. Bayout

Fig. 4:
Audrey's tree-patterned top.

pout her way out of the Norwegian catastrophe. But, once she steps out of her father's fortress, she chooses to show the world a different part of herself. Again, she's not just a young pretty girl; she's a fiery troublemaker, a sexy smart-ass in cherry-red heels – even if the shoes don't match her outfit. When some teens must live a double-life between school and home, it could be as superficial as swapping a tee for the tube top hidden under mom's flower pots (that's my story, not Audrey's), or as severe as Laura's unfortunate world of light and dark. The shoe change may be a clever motif, but the reality of it hits home for many fashion-loving fans.

The sycamore cardigan
In the episode 'Traces to Nowhere' (Season 1, Episode 2), Audrey slinks into the Great Northern dining room to boldly introduce herself to the new guy in town. Special Agent Dale Cooper is ordering hard-cooked eggs, cremated bacon and grapefruit juice, 'as long as those grapefruits are freshly squeezed'. It's no wonder that Audrey appears at this moment – and wearing a gem of a top. White with a black tree pattern, the angora intarsia-knit cardigan matches perfectly with her notorious saddle shoes. The balance of light and dark in both of these pieces represents, again, both her dual nature and that of the town. Meanwhile, the tree pattern reminds the seasoned fan of Glastonbury Grove. Could this be foreshadowing everyone's ill fate?

Audrey and Cooper's smouldering relationship is then ignited with that charmingly awkward conversation about his itchy palms and her dysfunctional family. Straddling the edge between teen lust and adult friendship, their ongoing tension is an example of a very Lynch theme – according to Colin Odell and Michelle Le Blanc, '[the] shadier side of human sexuality [...] in relation to a teenage girl'. Behind the scenes, it was determined that this relationship would never go beyond platonic, even though viewers' hearts yearn for the opposite. We just have to settle for the campy dialogue and the appropriate choice of music, while watching out for our romantic natures.

This image of a feisty young woman, a femme fatale, wearing slim-fitting mid-century clothes isn't very far from naughty pulp novels of the '50s. Collecting lustful transgressions between two covers, these paperbacks often beam with illustrations of Vargas-like women leaning in doorways, wearing negligees and smoking half-dressed on dorm room beds. If you've ever secretly slipped a tattered copy of a book like *Odd Girl Out* into your school locker, you probably understand why Audrey's look is so irresistible. One probably wouldn't find Donna Hayward on the cover of a pulp novel. Where have you seen a sour-faced girl in a baggy oversized down vest on the cover of a smutty detective story? Save it for *Nancy Drew*, Donna!

When fans share images of Audrey in the tree cardigan on their personal blogs, Tumblrs and Pinterest boards, they see a unique and beautiful find. This wildly patterned sweater is just one of those pieces you stumble upon at your favourite thrift shop when you have just enough money. You brag about it and you never give it up. The wearer herself is just as unique, exuding an intoxicating wicked innocence.

One might think back to an inappropriate crush once had, but vicariously act on Audrey's infatuation with Cooper through social media. We seek out her clothing to be like her, but actually living her life, the life of a pulp novel vixen, is just a fantasy.

Contrasting colours

Dream on,' Donna tells her classmate in the high school bathroom. She perfects her lipstick like a pro as Audrey shrugs off the insult. Giving up on her Special Agent just isn't for Audrey. She has major plans, and they're better than escape. 'Audrey makes it her mission to solve the mystery of Laura's murder, but not because she misses Laura, but because she desperately wants to sleep with [Cooper],' Fereiro claims in *Worn* online. Though Audrey does claim to have had a better understanding of Laura than most (during the breakfast scene in 'Rest in Pain' [Season 1, Episode 4]), it's as clear as her coffee is black that she's determined to impress the dreamy FBI agent. That is, Audrey has plans beyond the everyday high school student, and her wardrobe proves it.

I never thought much about her drably coloured outfit in this scene from 'The One-Armed Man' (Season 1, Episode 5) until I noticed how often it appeared in Internet searches. The cropped portrait of her from this bathroom scene appears on many *Twin Peaks* style sites as an establishing image of Audrey – her eyes wide, smirk forming, cigarette in hand, and a garish red zigzag wall design peeking from behind her. That red jagged line tracing the strawberry-oatmeal-coloured wall is reflected in Donna's outfit. Meanwhile, the red-hued wall really brings out the olive green in Audrey's clothes. This accidental or deliberate synergy between production design and costuming highlights each of these characters so well. Donna is wearing the same colours as the walls because she wants to blend in, she doesn't want to be different or weird. Audrey is the exact opposite, her green contrasting with the red zigzag. She willingly sticks out; she contradicts and makes herself a loner. That's our Audrey, having the nerve to take a smoke break in the bathroom as casually as she does.

Lastly, it's interesting to consider symbolism in one detail of her top. The sweater's lace panel yoke is like a veil of know-how and understanding over her bare naïve self. She's lured to leave the Great Northern by her own burning, immature need. Of course, she goes to one of the more dangerous places in the *Twin Peaks* canon, One-Eyed Jack's.

A double ensemble

Audrey's costume at the grotesque brothel in 'Realization Time' (Season 1, Episode 7) is a stark little black dress with a maraschino cherry for flair. The colour is bereft of her quirky anachronism – her lost-in-the-library brick reds and muted greens traded for the colours of high-stakes blackjack. Audrey has disguised herself in the skin of a sophis-

Audrey in Five Outfits
Angela K. Bayout

Fig. 5: Audrey's dark time.

ticated older woman, and gives herself a silly pseudonym, which is almost found out by Blackie. In a move so many YouTube users have extracted and posted for kicks, Audrey saves herself with her cherry stem trick. Oddly enough, this amuses the madam. While the trick is humorous and sexy, the viewer begins to feel scared for the girl, especially when knowing what will become of this 'Hester Prynne'.

Throughout her stay at One-Eyed Jack's, she wears a series of black dresses and negligees. This is Audrey's dark time, which she admits in her 'prayer' to Cooper: 'I'm in way over my head'. It begins to be too much – especially after the nearly disastrous encounter with the father she always failed at winning over. Though she's in disguise, this is nothing like playing dress-up as a child. Back into her regular uniform she goes. Wearing her rose-petal-pink sweater, pencil skirt, standard saddle shoes, (and in tears) against the blood-red drapes of One-Eyed Jack's, Audrey finally calls her Special Agent for help. The troublemaker herself is now in trouble, but as Blackie reminds her, 'You don't know what trouble is.'

The fansite TwinPeaks.org notes that Audrey's rescue is bookended by owl sightings. Just as Cooper and his trusted steed (aka Harry S. Truman) storm One-Eyed Jack's, an owl hoot distracts Cooper. He takes the drugged damsel to safety at the Bookhouse, while an owl watches on with wide eyes. 'In the Northwest, the owl calls out names of men and women who will die soon', states *American Indian Myths and Legends* as quoted by TwinPeaks.org. Could the owl be hooting out a warning, or is it not what it seems?

It seems that the fantasy Audrey divulged in the previous green outfit – the tall, dark and handsome stranger falling madly in love with her, taking her away to a life of mystery – isn't quite happening as desired. Forced into a heroin-induced stupor, then witnessing a murder, Audrey experiences a watered down trickle from the Black Lodge. Though her strength and determination shines through, Audrey is never exactly the same again.

Tastefully scarlet

Audrey's eye-opening adventure, her father's freak out (unforgettably lived out by refiguring the American Civil War), and his rebirth (save the pine weasel!) must have forced her to grow up over the final third of the series. Taking up the family business in the fortress she once ached to escape, Audrey's sassy outfits fade to business-grey suits. No more red heels or even highly suggestive schoolgirl saddle shoes. She's distracted from Cooper by the ridiculous John Justice Wheeler serenading her on a tacky picnic blanket. Her once burning crush on Cooper has cooled with her wardrobe. It's no wonder that fan coverage of her outfits during this period is almost nonexistent. Finally, after a rushed affair in Wheeler's private airplane, Audrey appears looking radiant once again.

Although she's crestfallen and heartbroken, her scarlet chiffon tea-length dress is a welcome return to her original saucy look. The fiery frock is either a reproduction of a '50s' evening dress produced by regional companies like Lorrie Deb San Francisco or Hi-Shop Baltimore, or an actual vintage piece. It's a special occasion dress that a teenager probably wouldn't have worn to prom, but a woman would have worn to a cocktail party. Hundreds of similar dresses can be found from Etsy and other vintage sellers, while thousands of women may be looking for that very dress to wear during a milestone in their own lives. On Audrey, it signifies her loss of virginity. This dress isn't the palatable sampling of red found in her famous heels, it almost overpowers her tiny body. Though she is as beautiful as ever in it, things just aren't the same.

Sitting barefoot in her scarlet dress before her father's fireplace, we see that she's been transformed from a binary being – an agent provocateur in schoolgirl garb versus a hyper sexual nymph – to a woman. As her first flame Cooper describes to his favourite Great Northern waitress, 'nothing beats the taste sensation when maple syrup collides with ham.' Indeed, the salty and the sweet create a unique experience out of two disparate flavours. Perhaps the mixing and blending of purity and corruption, light and dark, is what completes Audrey. Though her womanhood isn't all that exciting (like the mischievous days as a young pretty girl), she's compelled to shake it off and get back to work, rather than spilling some coffee and seducing an FBI agent. Either way, you've got to hand it to Audrey – she's not a weak bloom.

*****

One characteristic of a style icon is that she or he is regarded not just for enthralling fashion, but for a killer personality. The collections of images and outfit collages speak to the clothes, but what young women are saying about Audrey is uplifting. 'She's so unapologetic-ally crazy and cool,' writes the gal behind small blog *September and Friends*. *Rookie*, 'a new site for teenage girls', named Audrey as one of their 'Characters to Channel for Confidence'. In her 1990 *Playboy* feature, Sherylin Fenn knew how impressive Audrey was, even then:

She has made it OK to use the power one has as a woman to be manipulative at times, to be precocious. She goes after what she wants vehemently and she takes it. I think that's really admirable. I love that about her.

Her plucky and brazen moves cost her daddy's company a fortune, and made her a friend in Agent Cooper. They made her a goddess whom you would never stop staring at as she danced in the middle of the Double R Diner.

Something that lacks in Audrey-searches are scenes of her in the series finale, 'Beyond Life and Death' (Season 2, Episode 22). Bravely enacting civil disobedience, she chains herself to the savings and loan vault. Like Laura, she wanted to grow up fast, but she was too trusting and unaware. Allowing new friend Pete and his devilish brother-in-law past the vault door, she ultimately triggered her own demise.

And, you know what? I can't remember what she's wearing in that final scene.

For as long as the Internet lasts, Audrey will be emblazoned all over it as a cigarette-

Audrey in Five Outfits
Angela K. Bayout

smoking, saddle shoe-wearing, misfit in clothes that, after getting to know her throughout the series, became just accessories to her inspiring character. Audrey would want
you to dig through piles of musty-smelling woollens to capture the looks that make her
a style icon. You should do what she wants and continue digging through those piles
because, as she says, 'I'm Audrey Horne, and I get what I want.' ●

——

*Fig. 6: The author pictured
in her own Audrey inspired
ensemble.*

Chapter
3

Embodiment of The Mystery: Performance and Video Art Go *Twin Peaks*

Gry Worre Hallberg and Ulf Rathjen Kring Hansen

→ In this article we will address how a whole new genre within performance art has grown out of a fascination with the mysterious, humorous, attractive and uncanny universe of *Twin Peaks* (1990-91). This genre, born around the millennium in Scandinavia, but rapidly influencing the international performance art scene has, amongst others, been labelled 'interactive performance-installation', 'immersive theatre' and 'live and relational fictional parallel universes'. Furthermore, we seek to investigate the commercial spin-offs and fanfilms inspired by *Twin Peaks* that circulate online. Even though it's been more than 20 years since the show ended, *Twin Peaks* is still an appealing beacon for fans that wish to step into their own version of this mysterious and stylish universe. Commercial firms have also tried to attach a certain aura of mystery to promote their brands by alluding to *Twin Peaks*. Thus, this article particularly revolves around the topics of fan media and influence.

The most beautiful thing we can experience is the mysterious. It is the source of all true art and all science. He to whom this emotion is a stranger, who can no longer pause to wonder and stand rapt in awe, is as good as dead: his eyes are closed. (Albert Einstein)

The mystery in flesh and blood

'In a fake city built of plastics in all colours and shapes, a young man has escaped or just taken a break. He is the ruler of the city and he carries a secret unknown to all others […].' (From the performance universe *Desert Girls* by Fiction Pimps)

In recent years we have become engaged in a new tendency to use fiction in the framing of performance art works that we term 'live and relational fictional parallel real universes': fictional stories are acted out live in certain defined spaces between performers and audiences (or relational co-participants) resulting in the sense of being in a parallel, yet real, universe. Entering these performance art pieces has been described as walking through the canvas of a David Lynch film, particularly the universe of *Twin Peaks*, as if walking the small town's streets and meeting people as magical and enigmatic as Agent Cooper, Audrey Horne and Bobby Briggs in the flesh.

Thus, this new performance art genre seeks to turn the potential, that has been given life in the imagination of the audience as they watch the TV series, into real flesh and blood – an embodiment of the mystery, a deepening of the liminal potential (the liminal is at the heart of ritual as defined and categorized by ethnographer Arnold van Gennep in 1909). It's during this phase that the transformational potential of the ritual is liberated. When referring to the liminal, we refer to a space that differs from everyday life, which invites the participants to dwell in another dimension, allowing for another mode of being.

Betwixt and between

This new performance art genre is part of a larger movement within the art world that seeks to liberate or democratize the aesthetic mode of being – that is the emotional and sense-oriented aspect of existing in the world. This ambition is rooted in neo-Marxism and its dominating economic premises such as efficiency, duty and discipline to largely overpower everyday life in western society. Relational, interventionist and interactive art strategies aim at disrupting this domination – a disruption, which in our understand-

Embodiment of The Mystery: Performance and Video Art Go *Twin Peaks*
Gry Worre Hallberg and Ulf Rathjen Kring Hansen

ing, is intensified by the new tendency to frame performance art pieces in the fictional world.

Our hypothesis is that dominating economic premises lead to a continual need for 'special rooms', which for the remainder of this article will be termed 'spaces-in-between'. The term is based on ritual theory and the idea of the liminal phase as described above – a 'between and betwixt' (Turner 1969), which is understood as a mode of being where the premises of everyday life are put on hold and a sensuous experience is accentuated. When this experience is released, the world might be turned upside down. It might feel like a state of being between a world that is known and one that is mysterious, or rather 'betwixt'. This state is often used as a reference to describe the artistic experience, thus Bourriaud borrows Marx's term 'interstice' (gap) when applied to (relational) art works. Theatre studies scholars label it 'transitional' and 'transformative' (Féral; Fischer-Lichte). Spaces-in-between activate aesthetic, liminal and potentially transformative experiences (Müller-Scholl). The research on spaces-in-between extends to different fields of study, among others ritual, theatre and performance studies, that in different ways emphasize their ontology. Yet, none have specifically studied the new tendency to situate spaces-in-between within a distinct fictional framework: a narrative structure applied to a shared reality, as opposed to a non-representative framing of the 'ritual situation'. We will now focus on specific cases that illustrate a need to indulge in the spaces-in-between framed by a fictional narrative. And furthermore, how these spaces borrow from or are directly inspired by the world of *Twin Peaks*.

Twin Twin Peaks

Twin Peaks was a fascinating TV series. Its otherness constituted a need to dwell in a mysterious and uncertain universe. For some fans it suggests a need to act out their fascination with the series in order to embody it. *Twin Peaks* hit a nerve that drove people to impersonate, act and become one with the fiction that is *Twin Peaks*. David Lynch's series has spawned many fan-made media projects. As a base for this, the annual *Twin Peaks* Festival caters to the die-hard fans and their needs. It features celebrities from the series, a guided tour of the show's locations, and an overall celebration of the cult TV show. Of course, there is also a good deal of online activity as well. None of this involvement has dwindled, even though it's been more than 20 years since the show's final episode in 1991.

Among the most persistent fans are a group of thirteen enthusiasts who call themselves 'The Third Season Project'. Ever since the series' abrupt cancellation in 1991, they have been writing new episodes and discussing what could have happened later in the series' narrative. Finally, in 2009, they produced their own episode of *Twin Peaks*. The project is appropriately called *Twin Twin Peaks*, and is the work of dedicated amateurs. Their use of the original locations gives the episode an impressive likeness to the original series, and does an excellent job of

Fig. 1: Performers of SIGNA
embodying the mystery of
'Seven Tales of Misery'.
Photo: Eric Goldmann.

capturing the show's atmosphere by using Angelo Badalamenti's original score.

SIGNA

The performance art group SIGNA is one of the pioneers within the field of live and relational fictional parallel universes. With the immersive effect of durational and full-scale performances, the universes of SIGNA tend to have a deep impact on the co-participants, particularly for the performers that engage in the SIGNA-community by constructing the performance site months before the premiere.

Thus, over a period of several months, the performers engage in a liminal space where the boundaries of everyday life are put on hold. Slowly they become the extraordinary characters that inhabit this universe. Their bodily gestures change and they sense themselves becoming more feminine, more humorous, more evil, sweeter, sexier, more flattering and charming, or more controlling than their everyday persona. The performance-installation provides a magical frame that enchants everything within it, including the body. Argentinian SIGNA-performer Maria Pia Bertoldi describes:

> You have a mirror, and you look in the mirror and you think that what you see is the reality behind you, but it is not, it is another world on the other side of the mirror. This other world at first looks identical to the real world you are in, but it has a twist [...]. That opens up a whole new perspective on life. It's a different reality, but it is still real, and it becomes real – we start believing in it. This is addictive because the performer is inside of the mirror [...].

Thus, many performers have described their relation to SIGNA as addiction. 'I Need My Shot of Fiction!' exclaimed one of the performers interviewed by Gry Worre Hallberg, which is also the title of her master's thesis. This attachment to a fictional universe is well known to *Twin Peaks* fans. Our argument would be that the show is captivating because it inspires viewers to experience the mysterious within everyday life. For example, when you have your daily coffee break…

Embodiment of The Mystery: Performance and Video Art Go *Twin Peaks*
Gry Worre Hallberg and Ulf Rathjen Kring Hansen

Fig. 2: David Lynch directed a series of Japanese commercials endorsing Georgia Coffee.

Damn good coffee, and commercial!

David Lynch's take on a clichéd and almost exhausted theme of the police officer's love for doughnuts and coffee is so fun and lovable that it not only became a treasured catchphrase from the series, it also went on to play a significant role in attempts to advertise coffee brands around the world. Even many years after the series had ended, Agent Dale Cooper's face continued to appear in coffee ads. Dale Cooper, renowned coffee lover and endorser, has helped coffee companies around the world market their brands in many different ways,

David Lynch has directed quite a few commercials for high profile brands during his career, including ads for Sony Playstation (2000) and Nissan Micra (2002). But his Japanese coffee ad from 1993 is special in the sense that it uses his own art to endorse a brand. Lynch seemingly has no qualms about using his art for commercial purposes, thereby making his own fanfiction centred on specific brands.

Lynch's Japanese commercial campaign consists of four short episodes telling the tale of a Japanese man searching for his wife in the original *Twin Peaks* setting. Each episode features a clue that eventually leads to her rescue in the fourth episode. Whereas the series *Twin Peaks* takes it's time with nature footage and long and often odd dialogues, the commercials are fast paced. The main featured character is Agent Cooper, whose caffeine-induced dialogue rapidly discusses how good his Japanese coffee cooler is. It's damn good, apparently. The other featured actors in the ad are Lucy, Deputy Hawk, Shelly, and even the Log Lady, who ominously proclaims that everything Cooper says about Georgia Coffee is true.

The reason behind the commercials is *Twin Peaks*' huge popularity in Japan. Lynch was paid (probably very handsomely) for creating a pastiche of his own show. In using the original cast and setting for the commercial's benefit, Lynch is balancing on a thin wire between what is considered tasteful. However, seeing it now just makes for a good laugh, and it actually seems as though the cast members are having fun themselves. Lynch relies heavily on the use of clichés from ordinary life in his films in general; Cooper talking about coffee and doughnuts, for instance. But no one can twist the familiar and ordinary into wrought and eerie images like David Lynch, try as they might. The interest in linking a product to Lynch's otherworldly universe is fascinating. It suggests a need to transcend the ordinary and enter a space-in-between, coffee in hand.

Fig. 3: The performance universe of Future Minds Tours by Fiction Pimps. Photo: Inga Gerner Nielsen.

Fiction Pimps – 'The Mystery of Acorn Falls'

Whereas SIGNA work within relatively closed fictional spaces, Fiction Pimps, of which Gry Worre Hallberg is co-founder, instead create universes that transcend time and space to offer an aesthetic dimension in which to dive in and out of within the context of everyday life. For example, to frame the large-scale project *In100Y* by House of Futures, Fiction Pimps developed the performance universe of 'Future Mind Tours', a travel agency that sends travellers on guided tours in their own inner landscapes, as described in the seminar's program:

> Future Mind Tours is a Büro Reisende (travel agency) that travels within the human body and mind to dive into the conscious and subconscious world of the reisende (travellers). Future Mind Tours have facilitated the journey towards 2112 and have been of personal assistance to all reisende at the In100Y-seminars. The most sublime outcome of this journey is a mind shift in the specific reisende potentially resulting in a shift in paradigms in the external social landscape.

It is unique for a seminar to be framed by, and to allow for, the intervention of a performance universe. The effect is the precise creation of a liminal crack in everyday life that allows for a different experience that is sensuous and mystical. Furthermore, during the seminar, the knowledge production was, and increasingly became, influenced by the performative frame. Thus, the universe in this particular context was also an opportunity to experience and develop methods of art-based research.

At each of the four seminars, Fiction Pimps additionally tailor-made designs to facilitate different experiences of sensuous and mystical qualities. At the third seminar, Fiction Pimps, or rather Future Mind Tours, created 'The Mystery of Acorn Falls', a fictional filter applied to expose participants to significant events, and unlock colonized potential in their conscious and subconscious worlds:

> We welcome you back to Acorn Falls where there's always something in the air and the old oak tree stands firm as the spine of our daily lives. These days there are some

Embodiment of The Mystery: Performance and Video Art Go *Twin Peaks*
Gry Worre Hallberg and Ulf Rathjen Kring Hansen

strange winds blowing here and questions are being asked in the corners like, What is the final blow that makes an acorn fall?, Where does it land? and Who picks up the acorn?. Because as we say in Acorn Falls: The future's in an acorn.

Text in the program of the fourth seminar of *In100Y* reads:

Acorn Falls, strongly influenced by the vibrations of *Twin Peaks*, existed as a parallel dimension for the seminar participants to dive in and out of, but always present. It was truly a chance to meet mysterious personas in the midst of everyday life, a parallel dimension inventing the situation right there, creating an immersive effect where the participants slowly allowed for a mysterious experience to inhabit their minds and bodies.

For example, they had the opportunity to meet the character Pam at 'The Hourglass Inn – at the Waist of Time'. She would ask them about their personal life stories and a turning point in their lives, a significant event that changes everything. Many seminar participants opened their hearts to this strange girl who moved in mysterious ways. They might have felt as if they walked into a canvas of *Twin Peaks* and entered The Bang Bang Bar, a doorway to something beyond what the immediate eye can see and the routine of daily life.

Sophisticated coffee drinkers enjoy Twin Peaks
Another *Twin Peaks* commercial spin-off is a Danish coffee ad for Café Noir. This ad plays on a different connotation from the Lynchian pantheon of oddities. It is heavily influenced by David Lynch in style and narrative and does everything in its power to seem as odd as possible (see: http://youtu.be/aGHyuDG5m80)
A man is searching for a white rabbit in a foggy landscape at night, and the ad is shot in black-and-white. The scene is very stylish as well as mysterious, and mimics Lynch's later works such as *Lost Highway* (1997) and *Mulholland Drive* (2001). But again, *Twin Peaks* comes to mind as the protagonist in the story encounters a gatekeeper wearing a top hat and a cape, commanding the man to apologize to the rabbit. The music is ominous like that of Badalamenti's. The ad doesn't make much sense, but that seems to be the point as the final payoff is a caption asking: 'Do you think this is black?' and then a spinning cup of coffee emerges, once again linking the mysterious universe with the enjoyment of a good cup of coffee. Altogether, the impression you get is that of homage to the Lynchian universe, while linking the sophisticated art experience of watching Lynch's movies to coffee drinking. According to the Danish newspaper *Børsen*, it did so with quite some success. The commercial boosted sales for the coffee brand and won an award for best commercial in 2007.
The commercial even spawned its own spin-offs, as many people were exposed to

Fig. 4: Reminiscent of the doubles in Twin Peaks, the sisters Coco and Coca Pebber. Photo: Julie Johansen.

the universe of David Lynch through this commercial that aired nationwide in Denmark. On YouTube there are several examples of fan videos mimicking the commercial. (see http://www.youtube.com/watch?v=uDRG-hh_2tY)

This shows the effective attraction that lies in David Lynch's aesthetics: a certain hunger for a mysterious and alluring mode of being in the world, one with fiction and the experiences it allows for. These aesthetics are attractive in their stylish appeal and yet, they also reject any immediate sense to be made of the material. This leaves viewers pondering the meaning of what they are witnessing and invites a contemplation that is not usually offered to wider audiences. Withheld information holds people's attention, stretching the viewers' responsiveness in his or her own search for meaningfulness. For the hardcore fans, it invites them to act out their own version of the story.

Sisters Hope – Maybe you will be the next...

As orphans the sisters left what they had known to be their home and drew into the yet unfamiliar and unknown world, that, to the two little girls seemed infinite. With them they brought their most treasured belonging: their father's book. (The performance universe of Sisters Hope as described on their web- and social media-sites)

Sisters Hope evolves around the fiction of the twin sisters Coco and Coca Pebber (alias performer and Ph.D. Anna Lawaetz and Gry Worre Hallberg) who are also matrons of the school Sisters Hope. Thus, when the Sisters Hope manifest, it is an embodiment of the mystery of two twins and an invitation for everyone who meets the sisters to dwell in the same universe with them. Sigmund Freud points out how 'Das Unheimliche' ('The Uncanny') evokes the subconscious and mysterious through different effects, one of them being the use of duality and doubles (1919). In this way, the twin sisters Coco and Coca Pebber are clear symbols of something secretive and hidden, just as Laura Palmer and her cousin Maddy might be perceived in *Twin Peaks*, and just being close to them can be seen as a gateway to the liminal experience.

Sisters Hope very often work in a high school setting, and their essential goal is to

Fig. 5: One of the many uses of doubles in Twin Peaks.

open the students to the sensuous dimensions, a poetic sense of self. This dimension is also a liminal state, and as the universe doesn't dissolve after the meeting, it becomes a channel to access after the physical encounter occurs. The Sisters Hope also exist in a virtual universe on web pages and in social media settings. Among others, they send out letters to encourage former students of Sisters Hope to remember the embodied mystery and to keep the experience close to their hearts, in addition to reminding them that they have the power to dive in and create it themselves anywhere in their everyday life. Thus, this project also reflects on the exclusiveness of participation in the artistic experience. It is a democratization of the mystery, for everyone to embody.

Mysterious ways

Twin Peaks has had a huge influence on a very diverse array of media – be it performance art, commercials, theatre or fanfiction. The above examples are just a few of the many shapes this need to dwell within the mysterious and liminal spaces-in-between have taken. The persistent popularity of the series shows a need for the individual to enter a state of mind liberated from rational daily life, and for companies to link an authentic and enigmatic aura to their brands.

In this article, we have indicated that the inspiration that *Twin Peaks* offers points towards a continuous and ever growing need to allow for experiences that are not merely rational, that can't easily be measured or logically understood. Rooted in ritual theory, we call this state a between and betwixt that activates a more sensuous and aesthetic mode of being in the world, which might indeed be called for in a time saturated with the economic-rational paradigm of the twentieth century. ●

~~~~~~~~~~~~~

GO FURTHER

Books

The Ritual Process: Structure and Anti-Structure
Victor Turner
(Piscataway, NJ: Aldine Transaction, [1969] 1995)

The Rites of Passage
Arnold Van Gennep
Chicago: University of Chicago Press, [1909] 1960)

Websites

'Twin Twin Peaks', www.twintwinpeaks.com

'Sisters Hope', www.sistershope.dk

'SIGNA', www.signa.dk

Chapter
4

The Owls Are Not What They Seem: Cultural Artifacts of *Twin Peaks*

Andrew Howe

→ In its quirky characters and complex storylines, *Twin Peaks* (1990-91) hit upon a formula that would later be cultivated by other American television shows, many of them housed on cable channels where the darker side of human nature could be more fully explored. The show resuscitated interest in the paranormal, serving as a bridge between earlier series such as *Route 66* (1960-64) and *The Twilight Zone* (1959-64) and later shows such as *The X-Files* (1993-2002) and *Lost* (2004-10).

Fig. 1: Collectible mugs identical to those from which Sheriff Truman and his deputies drink coffee (via www.dudebox.com/blogs/news/6180762-twin-peaks-mugs).

Its idiosyncratic style and mysterious content resulted in unforgettable characters and plot developments, and the show quickly began to accrue the full sweep of cultural objects that often accompany a cult favourite. Despite the popular and critical success of the first season, however, the second saw a marked decline in support and the show was soon cancelled. During that time period, a loyal fanbase was formed, and lobbying efforts resulted in a distribution deal with New Line Cinema to release a prequel, *Twin Peaks: Fire Walk With Me* (Lynch, 1992). In this, *Twin Peaks* joined a short list of television franchises such as *Star Trek* (1966-69) and *Firefly* (2002-03) that, due to the size and engagement of their fanbase, parlayed cancelation into cinematic release. For a series that was cancelled after only thirty episodes to become such an institution is strange indeed, but it has continued to enjoy a high level of cultural penetration several decades after its release. This continued relevance is nowhere more evident than in the cultural objects that surround the show. It is in this arena of artefacts that the fields of fashion, economics and fan culture combine to create a richness of legacy, impacting popular media in ways that are both profound and lasting.

Indeed, the loyal fanbase has done more than just maintain the profile of the series, driving a primarily second-hand market in *Twin Peaks*-themed memorabilia, which has grown during the 20 years since the show's cancellation. T-shirts, mugs, calendars, character trading cards and other articles of popular culture continue to mediate cultural consciousness, impacting even those who have never seen a single episode. Many of these collectibles first appeared during the 1990-1991 run, although some were produced for various anniversaries, most recently the show's 20th. Other objects have subsequently been created by graphic designers seeking to capitalize upon continued interest in the series. The advent of the Internet made it that much easier for fans to buy and sell such items. The second-hand auction site eBay has at any given time several thousand items for sale from the *Twin Peaks* universe, many of them intersecting with fashion so that fans are able to proudly display their identification with the series and its characters by wearing a T-shirt or drinking coffee from a mug decorated with an identifiable character or icon. What has resulted is a market-driven proliferation of items that has served to advance the iconography of *Twin Peaks*, and perhaps even mediate which dimensions of the show have grown in currency.

Memorabilia can be separated into object type, such as articles of clothing (T-shirts and hats), fashion accessories (pendants and necklaces) or utilitarian objects (postcards and mugs). This chapter, however, will examine divisions based upon the object's con-

The Owls Are Not What They Seem: Cultural Artifacts of *Twin Peaks*
Andrew Howe

---

*Fig. 2: The wanted poster
of Bob as seen in Agent
Cooper's dream.*

---

*Fig. 3: In appropriating a
common phrase, the query
on this bumper sticker links
Agent Cooper to Jesus Christ
(via ozsticker.com).*

tent. For instance, objects that feature characters from the show predominate on eBay. One who has grown in stature among fans, as evidenced in his popularity in being chosen to adorn such objects, is the demonic character BOB. Although critically important throughout the entire run of the series, BOB had relatively little screen time. However, he has enjoyed something of a renaissance in online merchandising, perhaps due to his sinister nature and the terrifying, unkempt appearance of the line drawing displaying his face. T-shirts, posters, and other objects featuring BOB are common, many with the tagline 'Have You Seen This Man?' This drawing, a wanted poster of BOB that appeared after Agent Cooper's dream, derives from the third episode of the first season ('Zen, or the Skill to Catch a Killer'). Such a poster invokes the wildness of the nineteenth-century American West, where line drawings of iconic killers such as Billy the Kid populated local sheriff offices, and a spirit of general lawlessness predominated. A more sinister version of this poster, with the query 'Have You Seen Me?' can occasionally be found for sale. That such a character of evil might directly address the audience and break the proscenium wall gives a subtle spin to one of the more popular artefacts associated with the series.

Other characters also commonly appear upon memorabilia for sale, most notably Agent Cooper. Cooper is cerebral instead of instinctive, lawful instead of chaotic. He is not wild and unkempt, but instead neat and formal, something often reflected in the pictures used on these artefacts, many of which feature him in his trademark suit coat. In just about all ways, Cooper is the antithesis to BOB. Indeed, he is linked to Jesus Christ in a specific line of T-shirts, bumper stickers, and other objects that query 'W.W.C.D?' The fine print defines the acronym as 'What Would Cooper Do?' Considering that the phrase 'What Would Jesus Do?' did not achieve cultural prominence in the United States until the decade after *Twin Peaks* was cancelled indicates the power of the creative fan impulse, and the manner in which fashion items associated with the series remain relevant.

Laura Palmer, on the other hand, has become very much associated with the macabre due to the popularity of merchandise involving her character. Although a few items do employ her high school senior picture, including a necklace that can often be found for sale, most of the fashion objects display her post-murder visage. T-shirts, posters, and other objects have typically concentrated upon Laura's death, which has served to solidify her as victim. This focus ignores the fact that her character was much more

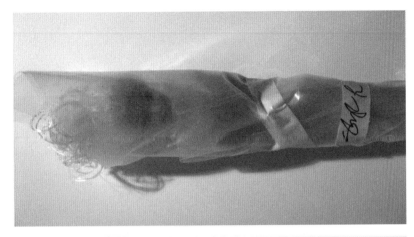

Fig. 4: 'Wrapped in Plastic' Laura Palmer doll, assembled by Paul K. Shimatsu-U and signed by actress Sheryl Lee. Photo courtesy of the author.

Fig. 5: 'The Black Lodge & the Red Room', porcelain Laura Palmer figurine made by Kiersten Essenpreis (with permission from the artist).

complex, especially in the prequel film *Twin Peaks: Fire Walk With Me*, where we learn a lot about Laura's life prior to her death. However, in fan culture, Laura Palmer is always portrayed as having just been murdered. Indeed, among the most highly sought after and valuable objects for sale on the online auction sites are the 'wrapped in plastic' dolls. In 1990, Mark Frost's assistant, Paula K. Shimatsu-U, took a Barbie doll, stripped off all of its clothing, wrapped it in plastic and then bound it in tape. This doll, which she hung on the Christmas tree at Lynch/Frost Productions, was so popular that she subsequently assembled a large group of replicas and had Sheryl Lee sign the tape on each one. These dolls typically sell in the $50–100 range ('The Laura Palmer Doll Is Back!'). In 2009, Kiersten Essenpreis made a porcelain Laura Palmer doll, placing it in a black coffin-like box filled with red satin. Titled 'The Black Lodge & Red Room', this art piece sold for $1500 ('Idiot Box Artwork').

Not all items demand such high prices, however. Due to the nature of the Internet and its second-hand auction sites, the market for the more esoteric memorabilia can vary widely. Even minor characters appear on the online list of fashion objects, and fans can proudly wear a Ronette Pulaski button, display a trading card featuring The Giant, or wear a T-shirt of The Man from Another Place doing his signature dance. On sites

The Owls Are Not What They Seem: Cultural Artifacts of *Twin Peaks*
Andrew Howe

*Fig. 6: Poster of Deputy
Brennan discovering Leo's
boots, designed by Brian Lenss.
Photo courtesy of the artist.*

AND IT'S ANOTHER GREAT MOMENT
IN LAW ENFORCEMENT HISTORY

DEPUTY ANDY BRENNAN

such as eBay, the popularity of a character can sometimes be judged by the speed at which an item is sold or the final selling price. For instance, a limited edition poster of Deputy Andy Brennan designed by Brian Linss sold out quickly, indicating either the popularity of that character or that collectors had not had many previous opportunities to obtain items featuring the clueless deputy.

Even characters that do not appear at all in the television series have artefacts dedicated to them, such as the often-cited/never-seen Diane, to whom Cooper routinely records observations on a tape recorder. A T-shirt is available that contains a hand holding a tape recorder, notionally Cooper's, underscored with the caption 'Diane…'. Conversely, Donna Hayward memorabilia from *Twin Peaks: Fire Walk With Me* does not appear to move very well at all, no matter what the listed price seems to be. Many of these items are promotional photographs from the film. Given its general unpopularity among even the most loyal fans, and the specific unhappiness with Lynch casting the bland Moira Kelly to replace fan favourite Lara Flynn Boyle, it is no surprise that such memorabilia is not highly sought after.

A common dimension of fan-based fashion accessorizing is not just character but also group identification. This is certainly the case with *Twin Peaks* memorabilia, where pins, badges, bumper stickers and even clothing items can help fans project a sense of belonging within specific groups or entities. It is possible to imagine oneself a deputy of Harry S. Truman's with a bumper sticker that reads 'Twin Peaks Sheriff Department', or to symbolically join the Bookhouse Boys with a pin displaying their logo.

However, fans can also ally themselves with the show's antagonists or institutions of mystery, evil and the occult. Wearing a T-shirt featuring the neon sign of 'One-Eyed Jack's' would identify the wearer with the seedy casino and brothel located north of the Canadian border, whereas purchasing and wearing the Black Lodge ring would suggest an allegiance to that dark location. Or, fans can choose not to take sides at all and wear T-shirts with captions such as 'Twin Peaks High School' or 'Citizen of Twin Peaks', the latter of which comes replete with population information. Unlike memorabilia that displays a singular character, items such as these are less about celebrating specific identifications per se than about establishing a desired corporate identity. The politics of belonging in fan culture has manifested itself more fully in recent times with the phenomenon known as 'fanfiction', whereby enthusiasts are able to enter the creative register by injecting their wishes and desires (and even themselves) into their favourite narratives. Pins and bumper stickers that suggest membership in groups found in the fictional *Twin Peaks* world are a slightly different, more consumer-driven dimension of this aspect of fan culture.

Phrases and symbols that derive from the series also commonly adorn such objects, and it is interesting to note that many of these reference the show's occult dimensions. The phrase 'The Owls are Not What They Seem' has become popular for inclusion on T-shirts and other such objects, and is a phrase that calls attention to one of the show's more mysterious motifs. Early on in the second season, The Giant gives three clues to Agent Cooper during a vision he experiences after being shot by Josie Packard. The second clue consists of this statement about the owls, birds that throughout the series seem imbued with an evil spirit. They are portrayed as predatory in nature and are often present during mysterious events that take place at night, including the disappearance of Major Briggs and BOB's escape after Leland Palmer's death. The owl would eventually become associated with the Black Lodge, the central location of evil. 'The owls are not what they seem' is an enigmatic phrase that has sold well due to its mysterious associations. The occult aspects of the series became more pronounced as Season 2 progressed, and the omnipresence of the owl as totem became a central feature of the series. Symbolic iconography involving this species has also played a role in fashion objects associated with the show, particularly as associated with Owl Cave. The owl petroglyph is commonplace on memorabilia sites, sometimes as its own decoration, but often as part of a larger ensemble of general *Twin Peaks* iconography. The map to Owl Cave can also be found decorating T-shirts. Much as with the phrase involving owls, the foci upon the petroglyph and the cave celebrate the occult. Such objects also serve to display insider status, as the symbol and the map did not manifest themselves until late in the series, after many viewers stopped watching. Such symbols, particularly when appearing without context or commentary, represent a fashion statement whereby a true fan communicates the fact that they watched the show through the bitter end.

Another commonly encountered merchandising theme that celebrates the enigmatic are items that invoke the phrase, 'My log has something to tell you.' The Log Lady is one of the strangest characters to populate *Twin Peaks*, as she carries with her everywhere she goes a log that speaks to her clairvoyantly. She often imparts pithy but confusing statements before exiting a scene, and David Lynch wrote nonsensical introductions for her to deliver prior to each episode when the show was syndicated on the Bravo Network. The Log Lady lives near where Laura Palmer was murdered, and with this phrase she indicates to Agent Cooper that she and/or her log may have overheard something relevant to the murder investigation. This is not the only phrase, however, that relates to the investigation of Laura Palmer's murder, and not the only one with mystical dimensions. During a dream, Agent Cooper sees a one-armed man (MIKE), who makes the following statement: 'Through the darkness of future's past, the magician longs to see/One chants out between two worlds: "Fire walk with me."' This dream is

The Owls Are Not What They Seem: Cultural Artifacts of *Twin Peaks*
Andrew Howe

critical for Cooper to begin to understand the mystical dimensions of the murder case he is investigating, but the popularity of this phrase appearing upon T-shirts and other items is more likely due to the fact that David Lynch used it for the title of his 1992 prequel.

Not too surprisingly, the intensely loyal following of the television series has resulted in conventions and festivals, where fans are able to see and sometimes briefly interact with the actors. As is the often the case, such contact has resulted in large amounts of signed memorabilia, much of which eventually works its way onto eBay and other online auction sites. A large portion of these items, at least those for sale, consists of photographs, some of which are stills taken from specific episodes, others of which are standard publicity photographs provided by studios. Still others, however, were taken on the set by photographer Shimatsu-U. Some of her photos were used in 20th anniversary exhibitions in museums throughout the country, including a still of Sheryl Lee with the myna bird Waldo perched upon her shoulder. When they went on sale, all prints of this photograph sold out within 24 hours, reportedly for as much as $600 ('Never Before Seen *Twin Peaks* Photos'). Not all signed artefacts are connected directly to *Twin Peaks*, however. For instance, Sherilyn Fenn has signed multiple copies of the December 1990 issue of *Playboy*, a magazine in which she was featured, due to her work on the show and upon which she appeared on the cover. It is interesting to note that the female stars from the series have a larger percentage of their memorabilia attributable to studio publicity photographs, whereas the male stars are most often associated with stills excerpted from the narrative. This tendency exposes an interesting double standard where male stars are noted for their work while female stars are marked for their beauty. These 'cheesecake' type publicity shots, bereft of the show's context, are nowhere more pronounced than with Fenn.

Naturally, not all of the memorabilia falls into the categories explored above. There are plenty of items that can provide for the collector a fashion statement of demonstrative allegiance without displaying characters, groups, symbols or phrases. Some involve the show's obsession with food, most notably doughnuts, pie and coffee. These foods figure prominently in the accessories that accompany customized Agent Cooper action figures, such as one created by Brave Workshop ('Twin Peaks Agent Dale Cooper Custom Action Figure'). For coffee, a fan can drink their beverage of choice from a mug that reads 'Great Northern', wear a T-shirt that says 'Damn Fine Coffee...and hot!' or warn others not to drink the coffee by referencing one of the show's jokes, where a fish somehow ends up in a percolator. Indeed, food is such an important part of *Twin Peaks* that several items publicize businesses that not only do not exist in real life, they never even existed on the show! These include T-shirts for 'Coop's Diner' (the Double R Diner was owned by Norma Jennings) and the 'Twin Peaks Cherry Pie Co' (Norma made her own pies). Not all miscellaneous items focus upon food, however. Others focus upon the surroundings and the environment, whether it be fridge magnets that display the entrance to the town, trading cards that show the Packard sawmill, or postcards that feature the local wildlife (for instance, the bird that appears at the beginning of the credits is a Varied Thrush).

Some items, although not strictly fashion pieces, profess to give the collector a greater insight into the world of *Twin Peaks*. For instance, a fan of the show can indicate their knowledge of its greater context by displaying on their shelf one of several books dedicated to the town's history. *Twin Peaks: An Access Guide* was written by David Lynch himself, and not too surprisingly contains some unusual flourishes. Readers can find out that the Log Lady majored in forestry and wildlife management while in college, and that two of her favourite foods are bear claws and broccoli (Lynch 1991: 33). Or, they can immerse themselves in the geological history of Twin Peaks, from the break-up of the Pangaea supercontinent 200 million years ago through the more recent period of glaciation, with implications for the placement of Big Ed's Gas Farm (1991: 54). There are even advertisements in this book, such as one for 'Tim & Tom's Taxi-dermy', an outfit run by brothers that offers both taxi and taxidermy services. Their slogan, 'We'll drive anyone anywhere, We'll stuff anything, even a bear', contains two footnotes, each one qualifying one half of the slogan: 'Within Twin Peaks City Limits' and 'Has to be dead'. Perhaps these characters, seemingly tailor-made for comic relief, would have played a role in the narrative had the television series lasted another season or two, at which point they no doubt would have entered into fan culture with their own set of collectibles. It is interesting to note that several of the official, sanctioned works fleshing out the show's mythos were written by family members of the show's creators. Lynch's daughter Jennifer penned *The Secret Diary of Laura Palmer* (1990), filling in the massive gaps that existed between the small bits and pieces of the diary that were used on the show. Frost's brother Scott wrote *The Autobiography of F.B.I. Special Agent Dale Cooper: My Life, My Tapes* (1991), once again building upon the scant information culled from Cooper's backstory, much of it derived from his interactions with fellow FBI agents Gordon Cole and Albert Rosenfield, or from the statements he recorded nightly for Diane.

A generation after its release, *Twin Peaks* still enjoys much cultural currency. The query 'Who killed Laura Palmer?' accompanying the lifeless face of a girl wrapped in plastic appears with frequency in American popular culture, standing as a referent recognizable even to those born well after the series went off the air. While contemporary films, television series and other cultural artefacts allude to characters, plotlines or bits of dialogue from *Twin Peaks*, the most relevant example of the series' continued popularity is manifest in the numerous and varied items for sale on eBay and other similar online sites. Fans can celebrate the series and indicate their likes and affiliations by proudly wearing T-shirts and displaying other objects. As graphic designer Brian Linss indicates, such objects link fans to the past regardless of whether that connection comes in the form of design or consumption:

The Owls Are Not What They Seem: Cultural Artifacts of *Twin Peaks*
Andrew Howe

I remember the feeling I had every week as I sat on the floor in my parent's house waiting for each episode to come on. I grew up on *Twin Peaks*. It was my first real exposure to actual artistic storytelling. It continues to inspire me to this day and I hope the work I create helps, in some small way, to keep its legacy alive. I have always felt that somewhere out there, the town of Twin Peaks exists. When I watch the series or work on a new piece, I am reconnected to it. I hope I can give something back to the place that has given me so much.

Posters designed by Linss, T-shirts that feature specific characters, and other items of popular culture associated with the show allow fans to access their memories and re-enter the show vicariously. A connection is made between past and present, between art and artefact. The act of displaying such an object is a fashion statement; one that celebrates political and aesthetic identifications and demonstrates the show's depth of cultural importance. ●

GO FURTHER

Books

Twin Peaks: An Access Guide
David Lynch
(Berkeley: University of California Press, 1991)

The Autobiography of F.B.I. Special Agent Dale Cooper: My Life, My Tapes
Scott Frost
(New York: Pocket, 1991)

The Secret Diary of Laura Palmer
Jennifer Lynch
(New York: Pocket, 1990)

Websites

'Idiot Box Artwork', *www.idiotbox88.blogspot.com/*

'The Laura Palmer Doll Is Back!',
www.jeremyriad.com/blog/toy-talk/the-laura-palmer-doll-is-back/

'Twin Peaks Agent Dale Cooper Custom Action Figure',
www.figurerealm.com/ viewcustomfigure.php?FID=26746

'Never Before Seen *Twin Peaks* Photos',
www.wired.com/underwire/2010/08/twin-peaks

Fan Appreciation no.2
Pieter Dom, founder and webmaster of
WelcometoTwinPeaks.com

Interview by Marisa C. Hayes

Marisa C. Hayes: What inspired you to start WelcometoTwinPeaks.com, aside from, as you so nicely put it on the website, 'filling the doughnut hole in your post *Peaks*' life'?
Pieter Dom: *Twin Peaks* rewired my brain. I first watched it at the tender age of eleven – recorded every episode and rewatched it at least two times until the next one aired – and the show definitely shaped my views on life, aesthetics, storytelling, surrealism, humour... Then in the mid-90s, I used to run a *Twin Peaks*-themed BBS (think of it as a dial-up website only one person at a time could visit) called Garmonbozia. Obviously, that resource died with the rise of the Internet, but I always kicked around the idea of bringing it back. In 2011, I finally bit the bullet, knowing that it would require a lot of time and effort to build an audience, and ultimately a community, of *Twin Peaks* enthusiasts. Needless to say, I enjoy every minute I invest in it.

It made sense to start in the same year as the 20th anniversary of the show, but even more so, I was inspired by its ever-growing influence on today's culture, from colour combinations in fashion, to samples in pop songs, to references in visual art. I felt the urge to demonstrate that even though more than two decades have passed, *Twin Peaks* is still relevant.

MCH: Can you describe your first experience with *Twin Peaks* for our readers?
PD: I remember it very well. The week the pilot was to air on Belgian television, our TV guide had the striking, blue-toned face of the dead Laura Palmer on its cover, along with the bold words: 'MURDER, DRUGS AND PROSTITUTION'. When my dear mum saw that cover, she ordered me not to watch it. Luckily, my parents were out the night it aired and my brother and sister, both in their late teens, didn't mind. The three of us were *mesmerised*. Instantly hooked. And when my parents came back home, we turned them onto the show too. It became a family event and we used to discuss everything that happened. Actually, to this day, we've never stopped talking about it. Only a few months ago, my sister and I organized a *Twin Peaks* themed flash mob at my brother's wedding. Yes, we'll go that far.

MCH: Do you have a favourite *Twin Peaks* character? Why?
PD: Dale Cooper is the obvious choice here. With him, Mark Frost and David Lynch created the perfect TV show character in every possible way. But at the end of the day, I wish Big Ed was my uncle. He's just aces.

Fan Appreciation no.2

MCH: What sets *Twin Peaks*' fans apart from other followers of cult films and series?

PD: I don't believe you can profile a typical *Twin Peaks* fan. If you ever attend the Twin Peaks Fest in and around North Bend, WA, you'll meet a very heterogeneous crowd. But I'm convinced I would enjoy drinking a damn good cup of coffee with each and every one of them. I'm always amazed by the extraordinary creativity of many fans. And I'm particularly excited about everyone using today's technology to mess around with *Twin Peaks*. *Twin Peaks* pixel art, for example, or Dale Cooper Photoshopped into the Occupy Wall Street crowd, or remakes of memorable scenes in The Sims. The unexpected, the mash-ups. I love discovering all those amazing projects and giving them the exposure they deserve. ●

Fig. 1: The Great Northern
keychain is one of the
products available at
WelcometoTwinPeaks.com

Chapter
5

'Yeah, But the Monkey Says, Judy': A Critical Approach to *Twin Peaks: Fire Walk With Me*

Scott Ryan and Joshua Minton

→ When we were wondering what we should call our weekly podcast about television, we didn't have to think long about which television show had the best imagery. We landed on the name The Red Room Podcast pretty quickly. We wanted the title of our podcast to let listeners know that we were not going to be discussing the same old, same old on our show. We wanted to discuss both the business and artistic side of television as one of the only forms of media in which business and art converge in a mass market of goods vying for people's attention. Throughout the history of television, the scale has tipped heavily to the business side. But every now and then a very special show comes along that delivers both, some even tipping the scale the other way, even if only for a brief time. Welcome to *Twin Peaks*.

Twin Peaks: Fire Walk With Me (Lynch, 1992) was released two years after the show *Twin Peaks* (1990–91) left television. The movie's influence on the entire series cannot be understated. It is both the last and the first look we have at that strange town and the mystery that lives in its woods, as well as in the heart of every human being. Fans' anticipation of the movie was huge. The series famously ended with a major cliffhanger: Cooper had been taken over by the evil spirit known only as BOB. The world waited for David Lynch to pick up this thread and move the story forward. It was unfathomable by television's standards that a series could end with the perceived hero overtaken by evil. That kind of ending is not allowed in American television. It isn't allowed in any popular form of American art. When news was heard that Lynch had raised enough money to finance a feature film for *Twin Peaks*, fans decided that Lynch would pick up the story where it had left off and that we would witness the redemption of Agent Dale Cooper. Any fan familiar with Lynch at all should have known that he would never do what was expected of him. Instead, the director parted ways with his television co-creator, Mark Frost, and went backwards. Lynch decided to tell the beginning of the story by show-ing the last seven days of Laura Palmer's life. This was the same information that had been covered in the book, *The Secret Diary Of Laura Palmer*, written by his daughter, Jennifer Lynch. Fans were already scratching their heads wondering why David Lynch would want to cover the same material that had already been discussed as background in the series, as well as in book form. The reason was simple: we can imagine that Lynch knew his version of the story held the answers to the cliffhanger. He knew that time was nonexistent in the Black Lodge and therefore time had no meaning in Twin Peaks. He was the one aware that all the answers for what had happened to Cooper could be found at the beginning of Laura Palmer's story. Most importantly, he knew there was only one true hero in the world of *Twin Peaks*. Only one human had ever bested BOB. That person was Laura Palmer, not Agent Dale Cooper.

Twin Peaks: Fire Walk with Me (FWWM) is a line in the sand for many *Twin Peaks* fans; either they get it or they don't – there is no ambivalent response. *Twin Peaks* fans can be assembled into two categories:

1. The Doughnut and Coffee Set
2. The Laura and BOB Set

If a fan falls into the first category, their lasting memory might be Agent Cooper eating cherry pie, drinking coffee or enjoying jelly doughnuts. These fans are more likely to brush aside the dark underbelly, and focus on the quirks and small town charm.

If a fan falls into the second category, they will spend more time pondering how

'Yeah, But the Monkey Says, Judy': A Critical Approach to *Twin Peaks: Fire Walk With Me*
Scott Ryan and Joshua Minton

Fig. 1:
From television to film.

Leland, a seemingly kind and innocent man, was possessed as a small boy by BOB. BOB infected his soul, taking him to a place that would lead him to later sexually assault his own 12-year-old daughter. Fans in this category are more likely to continually have nightmares about how innocence is stolen from children. This is a topic so horrific that it is rarely dealt with on prime time, and never as the main storyline. This was the story David Lynch brought to the big screen in his 1992 masterpiece, the *Twin Peaks* prequel feature film.

In 1992, critics erroneously viewed *FWWM* as a jumbled misstep. The movie was famously booed upon its debut at the Cannes Film Festival. With time, viewers have caught up to the master film-maker, and *FWWM* is finally being viewed by some as Lynch's greatest piece of art. His use of sound, symbolism and metaphoric storytelling will lead any viewer, who has the patience to let the art settle into themselves, on a lifetime journey centered around the battle of good and evil.

The first scene of *FWWM* is a powerful establishing shot – a running television with no reception that plays in perpetuity. We are not in the land of network television anymore, where genius programmes are ground into the dirt without apology. We save that honour for our main heroine who, up until now, has always been spoken of in the past tense. The television is on but nothing is there, and isn't this the most accurate depiction of American prime time? Suddenly, the television is brutally smashed with an axe; it explodes violently, extinguishing its glow. Lynch leaves no latitude regarding his feelings for television. *Twin Peaks* might have been born on television, but three seconds into the world of film, it goes through a dark baptism.

One must be knowledgeable about the characters and events of the show's two seasons in order to truly appreciate the nuances, and to dig deeper into the soul of the film's art. *FWWM* does not stand alone outside the *Twin Peaks* television show well. This is one of the main reasons that the movie succeeds. To try and make a stand alone story that ignored the 29 episodes before it would have been foolish. Instead, the series informs the movie, and amazingly enough, the movie informs the series as well. Lynch calls on the viewer to use their knowledge of what they already know, and extrapolate that information upon seeing the film.

Lynch displays this intention five minutes into the film when FBI Chief Gordon Cole shows Agent Chet Desmond a dancing girl named Lil. She dances in place with one hand in her pocket, squeezing her hand into a fist while making a sour face, wearing a dress with a blue rose. Chet looks at it and moves on. In the scene that follows, his partner, Sam, asks him about the dancing girl and Agent Desmond goes on to explain each detail of the girl and how they pertain to the murder they are investigating.

Fig. 2:
Lil, the dancing girl.

In this scene, it seems that Lynch is telling the viewer: 'Everything I show you matters and has a meaning'. He wants the viewer to understand that things which may appear crazy at first glance are actually vital terminology in the lexicon of his story. Understanding this terminology entails translating the metaphors and finding their respective connotations. This allows the viewer to begin to understand the story being told and the deep secrets held within, secrets impossible to convey with simple direct language. As Cooper says in 'Zen, or the Skill to Catch a Killer' (Season 1, Episode 3), 'Break the code, solve the crime'. This remains true throughout, beginning with the exploding television set at the beginning of the movie all the way to the shot of the monkey at the end who speaks the simple word, 'Judy'. Break the code, solve the crime.

Desmond explains that the sour face means the local authorities will not be hospitable. Her hand making a fist signifies the police will be belligerent. The other hand in her pocket shows they are hiding something. The dancing in place refers to leg work. The tailored dress is linked to drugs. The Blue Rose? He can't tell us what that means, leaving the audience intrigued. The jaded viewer may say, 'That is dumb, why have a dancing girl? It is weird just to be weird, even if they explain it.' But knowledgeable *Twin Peaks* fans know that Gordon Cole has a hearing problem and speaks loud. It makes sense for him to give directions to his subordinates through code. We can easily believe that everything in a Lynch movie means something. The aforementioned scene is explained immediately afterwards. This is the only time Lynch does so in *FWWM*. It is probably the only time he has ever done so in his art in any way. Using the dancing girl and the smashed television scenes as examples, we can infer that the parts of the movie which are confounding upon first viewing may lead us to a deeper understanding of the story. It's a matter of figuring out just what that explanation is. We can assume that Lynch does know what he is showing the viewer and why. It might just take the audience multiple viewings to learn how to watch a movie that is told through metaphors and coded imagery.

Once Lynch is done preparing his viewers with his story's MO ('MODUS OPERANDI!') he reveals what is probably the most perplexing scene of the film. Twenty-six minutes into the movie, Agent Cooper, the doughnut and coffee fan-based idea of a hero, arrives. Cooper explains to Cole that he is worried about a dream in which he is walking back and forth between a video surveillance camera and the monitor showing the camera's live feed. An elevator opens and FBI agent Phillip Jeffries enters. Once this agent appears, Cooper sees himself standing in the hall, looking at himself through the

'Yeah, But the Monkey Says, Judy': A Critical Approach to *Twin Peaks: Fire Walk With Me*
Scott Ryan and Joshua Minton

Fig. 3:
Dale Cooper's gift of ubiquity.

surveillance camera. This is impossible unless there are two Coopers. Viewers of the show know that once Cooper enters the Black Lodge in the final episode of the series, he is split in two. But isn't it also possible that Agent Jeffries is just a metaphorical version of Cooper? Here is where the influence of the series really comes into play; the viewer must apply their knowledge of the final episode to this scene, looking deeper into the subtext beyond the surface, otherwise the narrative seems ridiculous.

This is not a one way interaction, though, because this also influences the series, setting up Cooper's inevitable divergence in the Black Lodge, the end written from the beginning. It is impossible to separate the movie and the series from one other. The above scene starts fading into shots of The Man from Another Place, BOB, a fuzzy TV set and creamed corn. For those willing to spend the time with it, this two minute montage contains the answer to almost every mystery of *Twin Peaks*.

With a completely mad expression, Jeffries says, 'I'm not gonna talk about Judy. In fact, we're not going to talk about Judy at all.' This references a case that Jeffries was working on when he disappeared years ago. Viewers who have watched both the series and the movie know that Laura brings Cooper to a case that leads to the Black Lodge. Teresa Banks brings Desmond to a case leading to the Black Lodge and now Jeffries is distraught over Judy. We can extrapolate that Judy was his own Laura Palmer. He has either been taken to the Black Lodge or has a destiny there; the penalty for these modern day Knights of the Round Table when they can't save their victims.

Next, the screen fades to a meeting of other-worldly characters, some new to us and some from the series like Mrs. Tremond and her grandson. The Tremonds were first shown in the series, but at this point Lynch is playing with time. Just like the Black Lodge, viewers see the past and the future at the same time.

We already know Cooper will be inhabited by BOB, even though the agent won't be assigned to the Laura Palmer case for another 12 months. Jeffries also asks Cole and Albert Rosenfield if they know who Cooper is. Can we infer that Jeffries knows Cooper will be turned? As a final clue from Lynch, illustrating how important this scene is, he scores the theme song to the movie over the entire visit from Phillip Jeffries. The fact that the theme song is playing indicates that this scene potentially holds the key to the entire film. As illustrated in his body of work, music is critical to David Lynch.

Despite all its metaphoric pomposity, there is one character in *Twin Peaks* who never lies to the audience, is never coy or nebulous in its meaning – the film's music. Lynch never uses sound without a purpose, and the gorgeous music of the film and series provides the audience with a gauge that defines the emotion and truth of what is being displayed on-screen. This is one of the primary reasons Lynch is so effective as an artist – he doesn't rob the audience of all sensibility; he generally provides a touchstone of sanity through musical pieces, which accompany his portrait-like visuals, and at times

Fig. 4:
A smile for a smile.

frightening dialogue.

There is one primary asset the movie has that it commands over the television show: Sheryl Lee's performance as Laura Palmer, arguably the most fascinating narrative in all of *Twin Peaks*. If Laura Palmer doesn't die then none of us meet her. She has to die in order to bring *Twin Peaks* to life, and in many ways her death is a blessing, both to her and the audience witnessing the sublime unfolding of the events before and after her demise. Like many martyrs, she journeys through hell and rises angelic from the ashes, as the rays of eternity shine through her sacrifice and redemption.

The reason most movies are watched is to experience the end of the story and see what surprises the plot holds. But with *FWWM*, the end is known before it begins – Laura Palmer dies and Cooper falls. There is no ultimate saviour here. Viewers are left to infer, to hope and, ultimately, to doubt. The entire spectrum of emotion regarding this downfall can be watched, heard and felt in Sheryl Lee's performance, which we believe is one of the greatest pieces of acting by any actress on film.

Consider the following: Laura's crying jag when she demands from Donna to say she is her best friend; her amazing smile of innocence when she simmers an angry Bobby outside the school; her abusive and scary behaviour as she threatens Harold Smith; the time she loses all control as her father and the One-Armed Man argue in the car; or her seduction at the Roadhouse, where she can even make the name 'Buck' seem sexy. It is tragic that this performance has gone so unappreciated. *FWWM* was generally seen as inaccessible to the average viewer who bought a ticket thinking it was a horror movie, complete with linear narration and a monster that could be killed with fire. Instead, audiences encountered a non-corporeal beast who walks with fire, and a tangential storyline with obtuse imagery that often descended into plain old weirdness. But there is a reason we are still discussing this movie 20 years later, while those other monster movies have become Pez dispensers and greeting cards.

So why are we still obsessed with this movie 20 years later? Because it is art on a modern-day scale, one which uses the two primary media by which popular culture is ingested – film and television. 20 years is nothing to a medieval cathedral and it is merely a slight pause for Bach's 'Wachet Auf'. *FWWM* is a moving painting that deserves to be looked at longer than its running time. It can be studied and meditated on for the rest of our lives. Consider how Lynch chooses to visualize Laura's dream an hour into the feature film. She is given a painting by the other worldly Mrs. Tremond. Laura hangs it on her wall and lies staring at it as she drifts off to sleep. The camera jump cuts to the

'Yeah, But the Monkey Says, Judy': A Critical Approach to *Twin Peaks: Fire Walk With Me*
Scott Ryan and Joshua Minton

Fig. 5:
Trapped in a painting.

inside of the painting and starts travelling though the open doors heading towards the familiar red curtains. Cooper and The Man from Another Place converse about a ring, and Laura appears back in her bed. She gets up and opens her bedroom door. She turns around and looks behind her at the bedroom wall. Laura is shown standing in the very painting that hangs on her wall. She has been placed inside framed, moving art. Some might call that a television screen – moving art with a box around it. Lynch knows that Laura is the art that the viewer has been watching. He can destroy it with as many axes as he pleases, but the legacy will always live on. Laura will always be trapped in a paint-

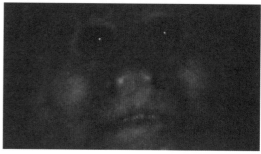

ing that Mark Frost and David Lynch painted, one that we can't stop looking at. This disturbing vignette is one of the most important meta-scenes ever captured on film. It is Sheryl Lee's acting that ultimately sells the moment. The ambivalent look on her face is perfectly chilling. She is neither frightened by this experience nor exhilarated by it. She is the true hero of *Twin Peaks*, not Agent Cooper. She knows her destiny is to die, to bring us something to experience. She is well aware that her future will consist of acting out a play over and over again inside a framed piece of art, whether it is a television set, a movie screen, or hanging on her own bedroom wall. Either way, Laura Palmer will never escape this future. She doesn't fight it, she accepts it. In doing so, she is the one person to best the villain of BOB.

Fig. 6:
The monkey behind the mask.

This movie is a reflection of a society that hides its darkness under small town goodness. We would like to go on record as saying that if you love *Twin Peaks* the show, but don't love *FWWM*, then you are not a true *Twin Peaks* fan; you are a television fan with a taste for weirdness. When you have allowed the entire expression of *Twin Peaks* and *FWWM* into your heart and mind, then *FWWM* becomes like a fine wine which cleanses your palate of all the superhero movies and dramedies that compose the bulk of what Hollywood churns out year after year. The film *Twin Peaks: Fire Walk with Me* will yield mysteries for years and decades to come, while never giving up its ultimate secrets, even though we know they are there, hidden inside the fabric of each scene awaiting our discovery. Lynch has led us to understand that each shot means something. Although we must admit that, for each mystery we solve, we still scream at each other saying, 'Yeah, but the monkey says Judy.' ●

[VOICEOVER]
SOMETIME IDEAS, LIKE MEN,
JUMP UP AND SAY 'HELLO'.
THEY INTRODUCE THEMSELVES,
THESE IDEAS, WITH WORDS.
ARE THEY WORDS?
THESE IDEAS SPEAK SO STRANGELY.
ALL THAT WE SEE IN THIS WORLD
IS BASED ON SOMEONE'S IDEAS.
SOME IDEAS ARE DESTRUCTIVE,
SOME ARE CONSTRUCTIVE.
SOME IDEAS CAN ARRIVE
IN THE FORM OF A DREAM.
I CAN SAY IT AGAIN:
SOME IDEAS ARRIVE
IN THE FORM OF A DREAM.

LOG LADY
SEASON 1, EPISODE 2

Fan Appreciation no.3
Low Zu Boon, Film Programmer at
the National Museum of Singapore

Interview by Marisa C. Hayes

In March 2012, the National Museum of Singapore decided to celebrate the 20th anniversary of David Lynch's *Twin Peaks: Fire Walk with Me* (Lynch, 1992) by screening the film in the museum's Gallery Theatre. The museum's website states that its World Cinema Series features 'works by the boldest and most inventive auteurs in the history of cinema'. Here, the National Museum of Singapore's film programmer Low Zu Boon takes a moment to discuss the film, and how Singaporean fans respond to the world of *Twin Peaks* (1990–91).

Marisa C. Hayes: What prompted your decision to include the film *Twin Peaks: Fire Walk with Me* in your recent programming? Are there many *Twin Peaks* fans in Singapore?

LZB: We recently screened *Twin Peaks: Fire Walk with Me* as part of our ongoing programme, World Cinema Series, which is a monthly screening of renowned classics, as well as neglected masterpieces from the history of cinema. It might seem like a surprising selection based on the films that we would generally screen, but we felt that the time was right to revisit this iconic piece of cinema and give our audience a chance to experience it on the big screen on the occasion of its 20th anniversary. Our programming is motivated not only by film history, but also the representation of history through film. I felt that *Twin Peaks* is a potent filmic text that figuratively encapsulates a stray trajectory of and beneath the American Dream at a certain juncture of history.

There are certainly Twin Peaks fans in Singapore! Even though they are not as prominent and visible as, for example, the fanbase in America.

MCH: How did audiences respond to your screening of the film?

LZB: *Twin Peaks* garnered the most audience this year for our World Cinema Series programme. Its status as a cult classic was felt throughout the event. We had our regulars and also a younger generation of film-goers who seem pretty enthusiastic about the works of David Lynch. There were audible discussions about the mythology of *Twin Peaks* and the film's intersection with the TV series before and after the screening.

MCH: What is outstanding to you about the film *Twin Peaks: Fire Walk With Me*? And how has the film weathered the test of time 20 years after its initial release? In North America, the film's cinematic release was a commercial failure. Was this also the case in Singapore?

LZB: The film is still a revelation after all these years. I find that it is one of Lynch's most visceral illustrations of the subconscious. Desires seem

Fan Appreciation no.3

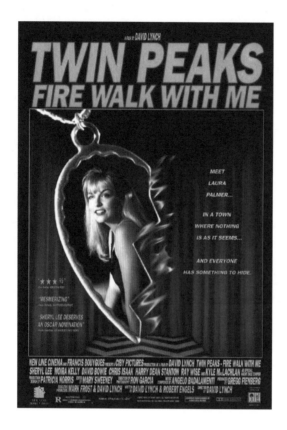

Fig. 1:
Left: Original US one Sheet
Movie Poster from 1994

Fig. 2:
Opposite: Bob collects the
garmonbozia in Twin Peaks
Fire Walk With Me

to flow hypnotically through this buzzing electrifying energy. It is horrific yet equally seductive. It is ingenious how Lynch mapped the effects
of repression, its lingering stain on the subconscious, how it multiplies
into a labyrinth of liminal spaces, doorways and a bestiary of creatures,
which soak up the horrors of reality, only to flow back to the surface with a
frightening intensity. It's quite a masterclass in horror! Furthermore, I find
that the film's pastiche of America in the '50s seems pretty out of joint to
begin with, giving the film a timeless quality.

I'm not so sure how the film fared when it was released in Singapore
back in the '90s. However, on an interesting note, the film had a brief re-
run at the 'infamous' Yangtze Cinema, a very interesting venue in China-
town, very much apart from the run-of-the-mill cinema complexes. This
is the only cinema in Singapore dedicated to the screening of erotic films
(drawing some parallels with the *Pinku eiga* theatres in Japan), and it

generally attracts an older crowd of retirees and the occasional film buff. On the other hand, the TV series was a different matter. Apparently it was well received due to the way it offered a new and unusual experience with the pleasures, and in a certain sense, guise of a soap opera. ●

Chapter
6

The Dream Logic of *Twin Peaks*

Kelly Bulkeley

→ David Lynch's film and television works have often been described as expressions of 'dream logic'. To me, as a dream researcher, that phrase opens up an intriguing line of inquiry. I take it as an invitation to consider Lynch's works in light of current knowledge about the phenomenology of dreaming. Many questions about the nature and functions of dreaming remain unanswered, but best available evidence suggests that dreaming is not merely random neural nonsense from the brain, but is rather a creative and meaningful product of the imagination during sleep.

This is why the phrase 'dream logic' is not an oxymoron. There is indeed a logic to dreaming, a logic that differs from ordinary waking thought but is neither inferior nor subservient to it—quite the opposite, perhaps. Dream logic embraces embodied instinct and cosmic self-awareness, our lowest animal desires and our highest spiritual aspirations, our darkest fears and our brightest joys. It governs a much wider range of experiences and realities than is normally recognized by waking consciousness.

Dreaming is clearly an integral aspect of human existence and a hardwired feature of healthy brain/mind functioning. But the autonomous otherness of dreaming makes it a disturbing phenomenon for many people. Dreaming is both me and not-me, and it's the latter element that makes people uncomfortable. They don't like the sense of an alien intelligence dwelling within their own minds. It's an insult to the sovereignty of the waking ego, an unwanted intrusion of strange memories and unsettling emotions into their awareness. This wary, ego-protecting attitude is then confirmed when people hear prominent scientists dismissing dreams as neural garbage.

This attitude persists despite growing evidence against it, which is problematic because it discourages people from exploring a powerful source of creative imagination that each human is born with – the capacity to dream, to imagine, to envision alternative possibilities, to discern realities beyond the boundaries of conventional waking reality. Dreaming is a human birthright, and people deserve more knowledge about their own innate potentials, not less.

David Lynch's works prove that some of the best and most compelling insights about dreaming come from artists who have the ability to connect with the alien otherness of dreaming, and channel its energies into creative expressions. The television series *Twin Peaks* (1990–91) offers an especially illuminating example of Lynch's dream logic in action. The serial format allows him to develop an extended network of dream influences and interactions unfolding back and forth through time and across different domains of reality. The remote wilderness town of Twin Peaks becomes a kind of oneiric playground in which a whole community is consumed and enthralled by the logic of dreaming.

Preludes

As the Log Lady tells us in her introduction to the pilot episode (Season 1, Episode 1), the many stories of Twin Peaks begin with 'the one': Laura Palmer. Her shocking death has given birth to strange and frightening new realities for everyone who knew her. In these new realities, the boundaries between waking and dreaming have shifted in mysterious ways. Prior to Laura's death, dreaming is treated as a light-hearted, easy-going realm of shared fantasy. In the morning before they heard about Laura, Bobby leaves the Double R Diner with a flirtatious, 'Norma, I'll see you in my dreams,' and Norma smiles in response, 'Not if I see you first.' Another example comes later in the pilot with the 'policeman's dream' at the Twin Peaks Sheriff's Department - an elaborate array of

The Dream Logic of *Twin Peaks*
Kelly Bulkeley

Fig. 1: 'I'll see you in my dreams'
(Bobby Briggs).

Fig. 2: Sarah Palmer, the unwilling
prophetess.

colorfully glazed donuts that Lucy creates each night to greet the Sheriff and his men in the morning. These references allude to the happy, playful dimensions of dreaming.

Then Laura's battered corpse washes ashore, and a much darker and claustrophobic tone takes over the references to dreaming. Ronette barely survived the attack that killed Laura, and now she is trapped within her own neurologically damaged mind, unresponsive to the outside world, her eyes darting under her bruised eyelids as if she were in rapid eye movement sleep, unable to escape the nightmare reality of what happened to her and Laura.

Donna, meanwhile, is struggling with ambivalent feelings about her newfound love with James. She learns at the beginning of Episode 3 that she had awakened her parents with her crying during the night, even though she doesn't remember it now. She tells her mother, 'It's so strange, like I'm having the most beautiful dream and most terrible nightmare all at once.' Donna's paradoxical sensation resonates with the integral polarity of *Twin Peaks* itself. From a rational waking viewpoint, a feeling like Donna's makes no sense. But it does make sense within the more expansive logic of dreams.

The worst victim of disturbed dreaming is Laura's mother, Sarah Palmer. At the same time of night when Laura was killed 24 hours earlier, Sarah lies on the living room couch and closes her eyes. She immediately slips into a clairvoyant dream of a gloved hand unearthing the broken heart necklace that James and Donna had just secretly buried. The pilot ends with Sarah's echoing scream as she bolts awake in a panic. In Episode 3, Sarah's fragile grasp on waking reality breaks entirely as she holds Donna's hand and hallucinates the face of Laura, crying 'My baby! My baby!' This psychotic rupture of consciousness leads Sarah to a sudden vision of killer BOB, the ultimate nightmare villain of *Twin Peaks*, crouched at the foot of Laura's bed. The intensity of Sarah's traumatization has exposed her to collective nightmare forces that are loose in Twin Peaks and threaten everyone in the community. In the midst of her anguish and loss of sanity, she has become an unwilling prophetess.

In the pilot and Episode 3 we already see the kaleidoscopic themes of dream and nightmare that will pervade the series as a whole. Dreams as expressions of sexual desire, as prophecies, as warnings, as doorways to other realities, as traumatic symptoms, as shared fantasies – all of these themes are already in place at the beginning of the next episode, the 'dreamiest' of the series.

Fig. 3: Agent Cooper, the shamanic virtuoso dreamer.

Agent Cooper's deductive technique

Episode 4 is the oneiric epicentre of *Twin Peaks*. It establishes FBI Special Agent Dale Cooper, the hero of the series, as a virtuoso dreamer and master interpreter of hidden signs and occult symbols. We already know from the pilot and Episode 3 that Agent Cooper embodies the paradox of polarity. Authoritative, competent and supremely well-groomed, Agent Cooper is also surprisingly passionate, naïve and childlike in his appetites. He is sent to Twin Peaks to solve a crime that involves a crossing of borders, spanning multiple jurisdictions; his job is to catch those who transgress boundaries. In Episode 4 we discover that Agent Cooper is in fact a kind of shaman detective, who moves comfortably through many realities and receives guidance in his investigations from intuitive, extra-rational sources of information.

This episode begins on Sunday morning, two days after Laura's body was found. Agent Cooper assembles the Sheriff, Deputies Hawk and Andy, and Lucy for a lesson in dream-inspired divination. After everyone has enthusiastically amplified their senses with doughnuts and coffee, Agent Cooper extends his wand-like pointer and flips the blackboard to reveal a map of Tibet. He briefly recounts the history of the Tibetan people and their spiritual plight in order to provide a context for a dream he had three years ago, which left him 'filled with a desire to help them'. Agent Cooper goes on to say:

I also awoke from the same dream realizing I had subconsciously gained knowledge of a deductive technique involving mind-body coordination operating hand-in-hand with the deepest level of intuition.

Agent Cooper goes on to demonstrate this method, which consists of standing sixty feet, six inches away from a glass bottle (the distance between a baseball pitcher's mound and home plate), taking a rock in his hand, speaking the name of a possible suspect to the rock, then throwing it at the bottle.

Most discussions about dreaming in *Twin Peaks* focus on Cooper's dream at the end of Episode 3, but I believe this scene presents a much more radical challenge to the waking world status quo of the show's audience. Agent Cooper employs a method of crime-solving that utterly defies rational analysis – or, more precisely, it extends the mind be-

The Dream Logic of *Twin Peaks*
Kelly Bulkeley

yond rational analysis to access other modes of knowing. His deductive technique has several components that must be carefully prepared, monitored and recorded, requiring a high degree of focused, rational attention. Yet the connection between the results (breaking the bottle) and the interpretation (being involved in Laura's death) cannot be rationally explained. Nevertheless, as the investigation unfolds over the next several episodes, it becomes clear that each of Agent Cooper's throws at the bottle is indeed an accurate indication of that characters' proximity to the circumstances of Laura's death.

In the middle of the scene, the Sheriff takes Agent Cooper aside and asks, with obvious incredulity, 'The idea for all this really came from a dream?' Agent Cooper smiles broadly and replies, with serene confidence, 'Yes.' The power of his dream was such that he has no doubts about the trustworthiness of the technique. The Sheriff goes along with him, perhaps because he knows that something more than normal police methods will be needed to track down and capture the person who killed Laura.

Agent Cooper's big dream

At the end of Episode 3, Agent Cooper settles into his bed in the Great Northern. What follows for the next six-and-a-half minutes is a phantasmagoric, multi-layered dream sequence that reveals in condensed symbolic form the final truth about Laura's murder. After this, the whole story unfolds backwards: Agent Cooper's investigation from this point forward is a re-discovery of what he has already seen in the dream, a process of rationally validating the intuitive knowledge of his dreaming insight.

The dream stretches and bends reality in several ways. It projects Agent Cooper 25 years into his future, when his skin has become lined and weathered. Some of the staccato images that flash into view relate to 'day residue' – things he saw the previous day (Laura's dead body, the bloody cloth in the train car, the flickering light in the morgue) – while other images in the dream somehow tune into Sarah Palmer's recent actions (going upstairs to look for Laura) and visions (BOB crouching at the foot of Laura's bed). Agent Cooper then hears the verses of a foreboding poem, recited by a one-armed man: 'Through the darkness of future's past, the magician longs to see/One chants out between two worlds: "Fire walk with me."' Earlier, Cooper had seen MIKE, the One-Armed Man, at the hospital, and he and the Sheriff had found a piece of paper at the crime scene with those same haunting words, 'Fire walk with me', written in blood. In all these ways the dream gathers snippets of evidence from the first two days of the investigation and weaves them into a bigger tapestry of meaning and motivation, a tapestry Cooper's rational waking mind is only just beginning to grasp.

But the dream goes far beyond merely repeating memories and scenes from the previous days – it becomes a headlong journey into the roiling depths of the collective unconscious. Cooper finds himself cast as the magician of the poem, opening his soul to the fire and the spaces between worlds, drawn into a supernatural ritual that invokes and temporarily binds the evil spirit of Laura's killer. Cooper gets a good look at killer BOB,

who acts as if he were surprised at being summoned thus. But BOB's violent energy cannot be contained for long, and he glares menacingly at Cooper (and the audience) and promises he will kill again.

Many nightmares end at moments like this, when the feelings of danger and vulnerability reach an unbearable peak of intensity. But Agent Cooper does not flee from the dream world into waking. A circle of twelve candles around a small mound of dirt blows out, calming the fiery emotions, and Cooper returns to where the dream started, in a room with red curtains.

Having survived the threatening ordeal of a direct encounter with BOB, Agent Cooper is ready to enter an even more mysterious realm of dream reality where he encounters two strange yet benevolent beings. One is a dwarf in a red suit, referred to in the credits as the 'The Man from Another Place'. The other appears to be a more mature and sophisticated version of Laura Palmer, wearing an elegant black dress. In addition to their distortions of size and identity, both characters speak to Cooper with a bizarrely unnatural cadence, as if they were talking backwards, and their physical gestures also seem strangely out of sync with ordinary human motions. At this point, Cooper is very, very far from the waking world and even from regular dreaming – and the farther he goes, the more he learns. Later in his investigation, he finds the waking world analogues for several of the details from this part of the dream (e.g. the red curtains, Laura's cocaine use, her arms being tied back, the presence of a bird at the crime). More importantly, Agent Cooper discovers that he has allies in the spirit world who will help him catch the murderer. He is not alone when he pursues BOB into these otherworldly realities.

He awakens abruptly from the dream, just at the moment when the Laura-like woman intimately whispers into his ear the name of killer. In the sudden shift from deep dreaming to waking awareness, so radical a transformation that it musses his usually impeccable hair, Agent Cooper forgets the name. Though we in the audience might feel a stab of frustration at getting so close to the killer's identity, Cooper takes it in stride. He accepts that he does not rationally know who killed Laura. What matters more is that intuitively he does know who killed her, thanks to this profoundly revelatory dream. Now

The Dream Logic of *Twin Peaks*
Kelly Bulkeley

Fig. 5: The dream suddenly turns into a nightmare

he just has to follow the clues to solve the crime.

The final nightmare

The dream references keep coming throughout the series, far more than can be mentioned in this essay, but all extending the themes originating in the pilot and Episodes 3 and 4. To note just a few examples, Agent Cooper has a brief conversation with Deputy Hawk about the 'dream soul' that can travel to the realm of the dead, expanding Cooper's shamanic links beyond Tibetan Buddhism to connect with Native American spirituality; Hank tells Norma that he dreamed of her while in prison, a romantically ominous wish-fulfilment about their comfortable bed at home; Shakespeare-spouting Ben says, 'This is such stuff as dreams are made of', to the new girl at One-Eyed Jacks, not realizing the girl is his daughter, Audrey, thus rendering his comment an unwitting reference to a nightmare of incest; and in perhaps the most intriguing dream experienced by someone other than Agent Cooper, Major Briggs has a 'vision of the night', distinct from an ordinary dream, in which he finds a way to reconcile with his rebellious son, Bobby. Major Briggs is a kind of warrior-shaman himself, more Biblical than Tibetan or Native American, who receives a reassuring dream of future family prosperity, much like the patriarchs Abraham or Jacob in the Book of Genesis.

By all accounts, the *Twin Peaks* series did not conclude in the way David Lynch would have liked. Outside pressures forced him to a premature disclosure of Laura's killer, and the timing of the final episode was dictated by the network's cancellation of the series, not by the intrinsic narrative development of the story. Nevertheless, Lynch directed the last episode and crafted it to end on a decidedly nightmarish note. After Agent Cooper has gone back into the red-curtained space of his dream and surrendered his soul in an attempt to save Annie, he wakes up in his room at the Great Northern, goes into the bathroom, and cracks the mirror above the sink with his forehead. As Cooper bleeds and cackles maniacally, killer BOB does the same on the other side of the mirror.

This is the final scene of the whole series, and it leaves the audience with a dark and distressing uncertainty. Has Agent Cooper finally lost to killer BOB? Is Cooper now possessed by his evil spirit? Has he gone insane? If a virtuoso of the dream realm like Cooper can't resist BOB, what hope do the rest of us have?

I prefer to trust Agent Cooper's dream in Episode 3 that he will still be alive 25 years hence. BOB isn't just possessing Cooper, Cooper is containing BOB, too. Agent Cooper has proven himself a man capable of the most remarkable integrations of polar oppositions, and it seems possible, at least, that he will find a way to balance the ferocious aggression of BOB with the mystical equipoise he has learned from the Tibetans.

Dream logic, reconsidered

Every dream-related phenomenon in the *Twin Peaks* series has some grounding in

current dream research. In that sense, David Lynch has presented a 'realistic' vision of dreaming in all its wildly numinous diversity. Certainly if we consider *Twin Peaks* in the context of cross-cultural history and comparative religions, the dream references appear entirely recognizable. In virtually every culture around the world and through history, dreams have been regarded as a primary means of connecting with sacred, transcendent realms, and certain people have the blessing, or curse, of a special ability to travel through dreams to learn esoteric knowledge about those realms, and bring back helpful guidance for their waking communities. Agent Cooper would be a familiar and welcome figure among any indigenous community, from Australia to Africa, from Siberia to the Americas, where shamans have served as cultural dream experts.

Even if our context of evaluation is contemporary western brain-mind science, Lynch's portrayal of dreaming in *Twin Peaks* strongly resonates with current research. According to multiple studies using a variety of methods, dreaming is fundamentally hyper-associational, perpetually veering between order and chaos, beauty and bizarreness, memories of the past and anticipations of the future. Dreaming involves a wide-ranging network of neural systems that are not bound by the strictures of waking consciousness, allowing for the emergence of novel ideas and solutions to problems that have eluded the waking mind. As many researchers from Freud onwards have shown, dreaming is deeply rooted in the instinctual nature of our species and the primal emotions that unconsciously drive our thoughts and actions. Jung and many other clinicians have highlighted conflicts of binary oppositions in dreams as symptomatic of failed psychological integration, while dreams of union and *coincidentia oppositorum* symbolize growth, healing and the emergence of wholeness.

Every night we go to sleep, we enter into a truly surrealistic realm of paradox, magic and ambiguity, where we learn, as Agent Cooper has so well, that our waking reality is only made possible by a beautiful yet precarious balance of mysterious, amoral cosmic forces. The dream logic of *Twin Peaks* is the logic of all our dreams. ●

Chapter
7

Twin Peaks and the 'Disney Princess' Generation

David Griffith

→ THE DISNEY PRINCESS GENERATION
In a 2006 *New York Times* column, 'What's wrong with Cinderella?', Peggy Ornstein reflects on her anxiety over the Disney Princess-ification of girl culture. She fumes over a trip to the dentist office in which her 3-year-old daughter is greeted as 'princess' by the receptionist and, as she approaches the dentist's chair, asked if she wants to sit in the 'princess throne'. Ornstein, a self-identified Second Wave feminist, snarls, 'Do you have a princess drill too?'

Ornstein's concern goes beyond the cynical realization that her daughter is a demographic targeted for billions of dollars in sales a year. She worries that this obsession with all things princess will somehow seriously harm her daughter, mentally and physically. She fears the long term implications of media and pop-cultural images that encourage young women to embrace idealized stereotypes of what they should look and act like.

As the father of a 6-year-old daughter, and a professor of English at a small women's liberal arts college in the South, I share her concerns and then some. My students frequently – and proudly – proclaim that they are not feminists. They see it as an angry, embittered way of viewing the world. So, in an effort to get them to think more deeply about feminism and gender in general, I designed and taught a course called 'Myths About Women: Gender, Power, and Violence in Literature and Film' for which I screened episodes of *Twin Peaks* (1990–91).

Though it went off the air in 1991, the cultural reach and influence of *Twin Peaks* remains astonishing: regular homages, newspaper commentary and academic scholarship debating its merits and legacy as one of the most innovative shows to air on network television.

As a David Lynch fan for many years now, I have been trying to find a way to teach his work, but could never find the right occasion. Then I stumbled across a 2011 blog post by Tevi Gevinson, the teenaged founder of Rookie, an online magazine for teenage girls and one of the hippest taste-making sites on the web. Her post 'Full of Secrets' meditates on her strange love for *Peaks* and Sofia Coppola's film *The Virgin Suicides* (1999). She admits that both shows make her nostalgic for her older sister's hip friends, and for the romantic angst of being a teenager. Accompanying her reflection are several stills from the show and film, featuring the décor of the Palmer's house (iconic photo of Laura sitting on a table behind a salmon couch with a doily draped over the back; an overflowing ashtray) and of the Lisbon girls' bedroom floor with its thick beige carpeting, tube of lipstick, eyelash curler, Polaroid of their house, a glass unicorn and a scattering of holy cards. What fascinates Gevinson is the aesthetic of these tragic girls' lives – a *mise-en-scène* that romanticizes their troubled lives. Their suffering seems glamorous.

Sue Lafky, in her critique, accuses the show's supporters (mostly male critics) of being blinded by love for its 'clever innovations [...] avant garde techniques, and postmodern sensibilities', qualities she feels distracted from its 'misogynistic representations of women and reinforcement of the dominant ideologies [of] gender, violence, and power'. Reading Gevinson's post, I wondered if young women were similarly blinded and distracted.

Despite its many portrayals of violence against women, I wanted to test my hypothesis that the women of *Twin Peaks* would provoke a deeper conversation about what feminism means to them than any of my previous attempts.

Throughout this essay I will refer to and quote class conversations and formal essays

Twin Peaks and the 'Disney Princess' Generation
David Griffith

written by students, all of whom came-of-age during the 'Disney princess' era, meaning they were born between 1988 and 1993 and were thus at least pre-teens when the princess marketing campaign began.

What we discovered, ultimately, is that the popularity of Twin Peaks with a new generation is connected to the evolution of Third Wave feminist thinking and attitudes from its beginnings in the early '90s until now. Twin Peaks, and its fan community, embodies much of the tension between second and third wave feminism right now in our culture.

'We are not born to contend with men'

To provide some historical context for thinking about misogyny and violence towards women, we first read Sophocles' Antigone, followed by Jean Anouilh's re-telling of the play, set in Vichy, France. In order to frame both plays, we read a chapter from classics scholar Sue Blundell's Women in Ancient Greece, an exploration of the ways in which the representation of women in Greek drama reveals deep anxieties Athenian men had about women transgressing their traditional roles.

Despite Blundell's learned and fascinating perspective, class discussion lapsed into talk of what a 'crazy bitch' Antigone is – the default thesis of many of the first essays of the semester: Antigone was crazy; she deserved to die. The correlation between her perceived mental instability and her death was not explored so much as asserted as fact. Why else, some argued, would she disobey the king's (her uncle's) decree? Why else would she ignore the pleading of her sister, Ismene, who famously reasons, 'Remember we are women. We are not born to contend with men'? Couple this logical fallacy with typos and grammatical errors and the average grade at midterm was a C-.

But students who were unable, or unwilling, to grapple with the contradictions of Antigone embraced the character of Audrey Horne. The popularity of a character like Audrey, whose image and motives seem to change at will, is a perfect example of what Charlotte Krolokke, in her essay 'Three waves of feminism: From suffragettes to grrls' (an essay we read in the class), calls 'transversity, a politics of diversity and multiplicity' that empowers and creates space for women to resist gender stereotypes.

In combination with transversity, third-wave feminism constitutes a significant move in both theory and politics toward the performance turn; a move away from thinking and acting in terms of systems, structures, fixed power relations, and thereby also 'suppression' toward highlighting the complexities, contingencies and challenges of power, and the diverse means and goals of agency.

Ornstein, who came of age in the 1970s is, without explicitly saying so, coming to terms with the performance turn through her daughter's love of dressing up as Disney princesses:

[M]aybe I'm still surfing a washed-out second wave of feminism in a third-wave world. Maybe princesses are in fact a sign of progress, an indication that girls can embrace their predilection for pink without compromising strength or ambition; that, at long last, they can have it all. Or maybe it is even less complex than that: to mangle Freud, maybe a princess is sometimes just a princess. And, as my daughter wants to know, 'what's wrong with that?'

Interestingly, once we started watching *Twin Peaks*, the students seemed to almost immediately adopt a Third Wave stance toward the characters. From the pilot (Season 1, Episode 1), they pegged Audrey Horne as a flirtatious bitch, but her attitude was not to be despised. As one student put it, 'we all know how to get our daddies to do things for us.'

The students who were previously very uncomfortable interpreting the actions of Antigone, now seemed at ease with the female characters who at times changed roles in a matter of seconds. In *Twin Peaks*, all of the women, from Laura Palmer and Ronette Pulaski to Norma and Shelley Johnson, find themselves performing in order to gain power or to avoid being harmed.

However, Third Wave feminists' embracing of hyper or, as Ornstein calls it, 'girlie-girl' femininity, as an option, an identity that can be put on and taken off whenever it is convenient or expedient, is not without its problems. Though arguably empowering, transversity and performativity have come to be perceived by many in the Second Wave and critics of feminism in general, as a step back, as a purely ironic sexual power play that aims to manipulate men.

As a result, Third Wave feminism is facing a critical moment in the court of public opinion and popular culture; one that is making it more difficult to check the spread of misogyny. The diminishing influence of the aggressive, tech/media savvy riot and cyber grrrl perspective that dominated the beginning of the Third Wave is a trend documented by Sara Marcus in *Girls to the Front*: the '[riot grrrl] persona has given way to much more accommodating, conventionally feminine images of women in mass culture.' She argues that the conservative political bent of the 2000s and a 'raunch culture' that encouraged women to embrace an overtly sexualized persona, sold to them by Britney Spears and *Playboy*, has produced a generation of more conservative young women.

From Carraway's perspective, a well-regarded writer in her early thirties who covers women's issues for a number of publications:

An ironic, apologetic feminism has replaced riot grrrl's rage. From where I stand, the 90s girl-culture revival seems to be more about blogging about clips from *Clueless*, not *Bikini Kill* videos [....] I'm wondering when girls are going to get mad again, because it's useful, and fun, and feminist, and not because it's cute.

In an essay titled 'Lynching women', written soon after *Twin Peaks* was cancelled, Diana Hume George admits to being 'seriously addicted'. However, after the show was

Twin Peaks and the 'Disney Princess' Generation
David Griffith

Fig. 1:
Donna, from ingénue to seductress.

cancelled, George came to the realization that contrary to Third Wave feminist commentators who saw the show as empowering, the sexual politics of the show are actually 'reptilian'. She goes so far as to say that the show perpetuates misogynistic views that will lead to further violence against women.

This got my students' attention. I had to admit that I was stunned by her conclusion too. To go from being seriously addicted to being repulsed by it led me to wonder if we were watching the same show. Personally, though I too was addicted to the show, I was nevertheless made nervous by the sexual violence, especially the scene where Leland Palmer, possessed by BOB, brutally beats and kills Maddy.

Many of my students cried foul at her logic: that the very process of 'masculine enculturation' that all men go through in the West, which includes the consumptions of thousands of portrayals of violent acts towards women, leads to 'lowered sensitivity' and attitude change with regards to violence against women. I agreed with them that the logic of George's claim is challenging, because it is founded on one of the biggest controversies of the digital age: does the viewing of media violence – in this case, sexual violence against women – make one more likely to be violent?

Add to this the fact that most of them were still wary of feminism – the term conjured up angry man-haters and bra burnings – and the idea that a television show could be blamed for high rates of violence against women was difficult, and in some cases impossible, for them to accept. One student said dismissively, 'If you looked at the world in that way all the time, you would be really sad.' In other words, even reflecting on the ways in which our popular culture might promote or excuse violence against women is depressing and thus not worth doing.

Caroline Ladson, another student in the class, took issue with George in much the same way a young Third Waver would take issue with Peggy Ornstein:

Could it be that *Twin Peaks* has created a character capable of both saddle shoes and red heels? George argues that a flaw of *Twin Peaks* is that it 'breaks women in half'. On the contrary, I believe that the ability of *Twin Peaks* to cast light on the different and drastic layers of its females' desires, drives, ambitions, intentions, and expectations, depending on the situation, is one of its greatest strengths. That Donna can switch from 'ingénue to seductress overnight' adds to the depth of the show because it was not a move that we the viewers had been able to preempt.

Ladson's assessment of Audrey embodies the best of what transversity can do as a theoretical framework. She sees depth and willfulness in Audrey's behaviour, not an empty-headed surrender to behave in whatever ways will best attract men.

Ladson makes a compelling argument for *Twin Peaks* as a show that dramatizes the

Fig. 2: Audrey Horne's complex character.

situation of young women in the early days of the Third
Wave. Ladson writes:

Could it be that this [Audrey?] character, so far defined only
by the death of her classmate, is made up of much more?
Lynch created a character that is already so complex, this
defining moment of the show affects only her actions
instead of her essence. Audrey is already her own person
within the confines of *Twin Peaks* and will continue being
her own person, whether Laura Palmer washes up wrapped
in a tarp or not. Immediately, we see a side to Audrey that
stands in contrast to our preconceived notions of her.

The struggle to be one's 'own person' is a constant concern for young people who are on the cusp of adulthood,
and so essays like George's and Krolokke's can be (were)
perceived as threats to one's sense of identity. The very
notion of a feminist critique rings falsely to many students
because such an action is seen as a foolish fabrication, a manipulation of popular culture to suit one's agenda. There is no rift between the sexes, they say, or if there is, it is
because it has been created by man-hating feminists.

Student Erin Whiteman points out in her essay 'Feminist *Twin Peaks*' that the beginning of the Third Wave of feminism (late '80s to early '90s) intersects with the debut of
Twin Peaks in important ways. Citing Charlotte Krolokke's 'Three waves of feminism:
From suffragettes to grrls', Whiteman writes that '*Twin Peaks* served as a form of social
commentary that displayed the differences within the umbrella term of feminism by
representing each wave of thought within its female characters and storylines.'

Unlike other students in the class, Ladson and Whiteman stay away from castigating
George; instead, they are able to turn their analyses toward a conversation with George
similar to the one Peggy Ornstein has with her daughter.

Ladson does find common ground with George, agreeing with her observation that
at the heart of the show is a battle between lightness and darkness in which darkness
wins. Ladson, an international studies major, likens the threat of the evil to that of rogue
states: there is something out there that wants to harm us, and it will not go away even
if we ignore it – especially if we ignore it. And that something is, as Albert Rosenfeld
theorizes, 'the evil that men do'.

Here, in rural Sweet Briar, Virginia, most of us do not feel threats from the outside
world. Certainly not from a world as far abstracted and removed as *Twin Peaks* is. *Twin
Peaks* undermines our belief that, here in our home, we are safe. The basal darkness
of human nature as portrayed by the show goes beyond the abilities of campus safety,

Twin Peaks and the 'Disney Princess' Generation
David Griffith

Fig. 3:
Ready to serve.

locked dorms or watchful eyes. It is an upsettingly vivid depiction of human desires, normally suppressed and groomed so as to be suitable for the viewing of others. The difference here, though, is that we cannot affect the outcome of *Twin Peaks* as we can affect the outcome of our day-to-day lives, making *Twin Peaks* an even more uncontrollable story line.

Digital Lynching

To begin the second half of the semester, we took to Tumblr and found images that provided insight into the ways in which *Twin Peaks* was discussed in the media while on the air. We found the 1990 *Esquire* cover, featuring Sheryl Lee, very much alive, but still wrapped in plastic as her dead character was at the beginning of Episode 1.

That same year, *Rolling Stone* ran a sultry cover of *Peaks* stars Lara Flynn Boyle (Donna Hayward), Sherilyn Fenn (Audrey Horne) and Mädchen Amick (Shelley Johnson). The women are posed in matching tight-fitting tank tops and blue jeans, and suggestively embrace one another, pulling at each other's clothes: Fenn has her hand in the back pocket of Amick's jeans; Flynn Boyle and Amick tug at one another's belt loops.

I posted these cover images to the class Tumblr blog (mythicalwomen.tumblr.com), and asked the students to reflect on the impression they conveyed. What would they guess the show was about, based purely on these images? The consensus was that the show focused on a group of promiscuous young women, which is, of course, not in any way the character of the show. This was a marketing strategy designed to tap into heterosexual male fantasies.

According to Zoe Cosker, who runs the popular Tumblr blog 'Twinpeaks4eva', there are dozens of *Twin Peaks*-themed Tumblr blogs, creating a community that shares images from the show back and forth, almost like trading cards. Cosker said in an interview that she believes 'the Tumblr reaction is more sexist than the original show. The way in which the "wrapped in plastic" image of Laura is reblogged seems sort of fetishistic and does make me uncomfortable.' 'On the other hand.' Cosker writes:

[...] the show does pass the Bechdel Test [includes at least two women; who have at least one conversation; about something other than a man or men]. And I do think it offers a range of female characters who are complex individuals. [...] [T]he popularity on Tumblr of Audrey specifically says something about how young women relate to her somewhere between teenage girl and adult woman, somewhere between really innocent and very knowing, and bold as hell.

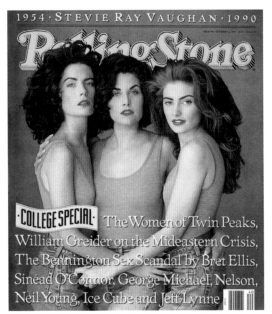

Fig. 4:
A heterosexual male fantasy.

Kaitlyn Dobson, another student in my class, in her essay 'Misogynist memes (No, I will not make you a sandwich)', traces the path of an Internet meme, from its beginnings on a site like reddit or 4chan to Facebook and its 175 million North American users: 'So, the idea that a woman's place is in the kitchen, and that this role is desirable, is now reaching 175 million people.' Even what are considered fringe ideas espoused on a remote corner of the web can gain an enormous audience within a matter of hours, if not minutes.

Put this way, the real concern, then, becomes the way technology is deployed to make misogynistic ideologies ubiquitous and persistent. Dobson's assessment is in line with feminist sociologist Kimberlé Krenshaw's theory of intersectionality, in which various forms of prejudice and bigotry intersect in order to create a culturally pervasive atmosphere of oppression.

However, here again we are confronted with another version of the highly contested causal logic Diana Hume George relies on; that there is a connection between seemingly hateful representations/utterances and actions.

So my students' position is not completely unfounded. For years social scientists have tried to find a connection between exposure to media violence and violent acts with no luck. In 1967, Jack Valenti, head of the Motion Picture Association of America for over thirty years, defended the film industry by citing this lack of hard evidence during his testimony before a government commission on the prevention of violence.

In 1999, Henry Jenkins, one of the foremost media studies scholar in the world, sat before a congressional hearing spurred by the Columbine school shootings and defended violent video games by again citing the same history of scientific studies.

Jenkins suggests that violent representations and images are 'complex bundles of often contradictory meanings that can yield an enormous range of different responses from the people who consume them'. Unintentionally, Jenkins is providing those of us living in the late Third Wave with a way of reflecting on the current personalist bent of feminism, which often seems contradictory, and can be both defended against Second Wave critics while simultaneously issuing a warning.

But how should young women live within this uncertainty?

This is where Second Wave critics like Diana Hume George, Sue Latky and Anne Owens Weekes are necessary, as their work serves as a guide to Third Wavers who lack historical perspective. With their help, young women can begin to see the duplicity of female characters in dramas like *Twin Peaks*, and that the violence done to them does not just affect the way men see women, but the way women see themselves. They will be able to see that the performance turn, though it seems to them like empowerment

Twin Peaks and the 'Disney Princess' Generation
David Griffith

through choice, is not necessarily a whimsical decision, but one borne out of survival in a world where historically women who transgress traditional boundaries are threatened with violence.

It's my hope that though they may not care for the politics of feminism, questioning the violence before them on the many screens that pervade their lives does not make them a 'crazy bitch'; it puts them in a position to protect themselves and advocate for the Laura Palmers of the world. ●

~~~~~~~~~~~~~~

GO FURTHER

Extracts/Essays/Articles

'Gender, power and culture in the televisual world of *Twin Peaks*: A feminist critique'
Sue Lafky
In *Journal of Film and Video* (51), 2000, pp. 5–19.

'Lynching women'
Diana Hume George
In David Lavery (ed.). *Full of Secrets: Critical Approaches to Twin Peaks* (Detroit: Wayne State University Press, 1995)

Websites

'She's Full of Secrets', www.thestylerookie.com/2011/04/shes-full-of-secrets.html
'Twinpeaks4eva', www.Twinpeaks4eva.tumblr.com

Chapter 8

Bond on Bond: Laura Palmer and Agent Cooper in *Twin Peaks*

David Bushman

→ Duality – the notion of doubling, or symmetry – is a prominent motif in *Twin Peaks*, the genre-bending masterpiece from creators David Lynch and Mark Frost, as suggested by the title itself: the Black and White Lodges; the depiction of the evil spirit BOB as the mirror image of his host body; the subversive light-dark dichotomy contrasting Laura Palmer with both her best friend, Donna Hayward, and her identical cousin, Maddy Ferguson (a hybrid name invoking two characters from Alfred Hitchcock's 1958 film *Vertigo*, which itself pivots on duplexity and duplicity); the use of palindromes (like 'Wow, BOB, wow', a line spoken by the diminutive Man from Another Place, or the name BOB itself); FBI Agent Dale Cooper's calamitous confrontation with his doppelgänger in the Red Room in the series finale – all are among the many illustrations of this theme at work.

This fetishistic preoccupation serves multiple purposes, ultimately setting the stage for a cosmic battle between good and evil, but also confusing the distinction between reality and appearance, a propitious circumstance in a television drama hinging on the resolution of a murder mystery (hence, the oft-quoted line 'The owls are not what they seem', spoken by a beneficent giant who appears to Cooper in a vision, or Annie Blackburn's invocation of Werner Heisenberg's observation that 'What we observe is not nature itself, but nature exposed to our method of questioning'). This chapter, however, focuses specifically on the duality involving Laura Palmer and Agent Cooper – two characters who, on one level, represent confrontational strains of a common narrative (one symbolizing obscuration, the other truth), yet who share a bond so profound that they experience the same dream, and appear to each other in visions even before either is aware of the other's existence.

Lynch, a trained abstract expressionist painter, who has developed a reputation as one of America's premier film-makers thanks to films like *The Elephant Man* (1980), *Blue Velvet* (1986), and *Mulholland Drive* (2001), has long been intrigued by balance and contrast, as evidenced by the appellation bestowed upon his production company, Asymmetrical Productions. In the 2005 book *Lynch on Lynch*, the film-maker told Chris Rodley, 'We're all striving for balance, in my mind. It's the ultimate goal. And it's such a heavy thing, you know, perfect balance. I think a kind of euphoria comes out of a perfect balance.' This motif is similarly addressed in 'I See Myself,' a self-portrait Lynch completed in 1992, the year following the demise of *Twin Peaks* the television series, though the same year that the Lynch-directed *Twin Peaks: Fire Walk With Me*, the prequel to the series, was released in movie theatres. Prompted by Rodley to interpret the painting, and its depiction of a half-white, half-black figure, Lynch replied:

Well, we all have at least two sides. One of the things I've heard is that our trip through life is to gain divine mind through knowledge and experience of combined opposites, and that's our trip. The world we live in is a world of opposites. And to reconcile those two opposing things is the trick.

Rodley: Are they opposed, in the sense that one is good and the other is bad?
Lynch: Well, it has to be that way. I don't know why (laughs) but um . . . er . . . just opposites, you know, that's all. And then that means there's something in the middle. And the middle isn't a compromise, it's, like, the power of both

This quote offers an intriguing framework within which to deconstruct the relation-

Bond on Bond: Laura Palmer and Agent Cooper in *Twin Peaks*
David Bushman

Fig. 1: Ronnette Pulaski stumbles across the state line.

ship between Laura Palmer (portrayed by Sheryl Lee) and Agent Dale Cooper (Kyle MacLachlan), who are functional opposites due to their respective roles in the narrative, yet nevertheless share a profound connection, partly for otherworldly reasons beyond our full comprehension, but also because of their common histories of deep emotional trauma.

Driving Miss Narrative

Laura and Cooper are the primary narrative motivators of the first arc of *Twin Peaks*, which ends with 'Arbitrary Law' (Season 2, Episode 9), in which Leland Palmer (Ray Wise) is apprehended as the murderer of his daughter, Laura, although it is revealed that Leland was acting under the influence of the demonic BOB (Frank Silva), who had taken possession of his body decades earlier. Although Laura is deceased even before the series opens - indeed, the story erupts with the discovery of her bloated corpse along the riverbank by Pete Martell (Jack Nance) while on a morning fishing trip - Lynch told Rodley (in reference to both the actress Lee and the character she played), 'One day she was there, and the next day she was gone, but she was in every scene mentally.'

Cooper arrives in Twin Peaks approximately one-third of the way into the pilot (Season 1, Episode 1); while technically it is the fact that Ronnette Pulaski (Phoebe Augustine), Laura's companion in debauchery on the final night of her life, stumbled across the state line in a fugue state after witnessing the onset of Laura's torment that summons Cooper to town, his primary focus once he arrives is on unravelling the mystery of Laura's murder. As we will learn later on in *Twin Peaks: Fire Walk With Me* (Lynch, 1992), the bulk of which unfolds in the days leading up to Laura's death, Cooper already shares a deep, mystical connection with the victim: while investigating the murder of Teresa Banks (Pamela Gidley), a 17-year-old drifter killed by Leland/BOB in nearby Deer Mountain, Washington, a year earlier, Cooper tells FBI forensic analyst Albert Rosenfield (Miguel Ferrer), 'Lately I've been filled with the knowledge that the killer will strike again, but because it's just a feeling I am powerless to stop it.' To test the veracity of Cooper's premonition, Albert peppers him with questions - Will the next victim be a man or woman? What colour hair does she have? - Cooper's answers to which all prove prescient. 'She's in high school,' Cooper says. 'She is sexually active. She's using drugs. She's crying out for help.' When Albert - frustrated by Cooper's lack of specificity - inquires as to what she is doing at that exact moment, Cooper replies, 'She's preparing a great abundance of food,' at which point the camera cuts to Laura at the Double R Diner in Twin Peaks, gearing up for a Meals on Wheels run.

Later in *Twin Peaks: Fire Walk With Me*, these roles are reversed, when it is Laura who has a vision of Cooper - a man she has never met and whose existence she has no knowledge of - in a dream that unfolds in the so-called Red Room. During this dream, The Man from Another Place (Michael J. Anderson) offers Laura a green ring with cave

Fig. 2: The Man from Another Place offers a ring to Laura.

markings that had once belonged to Teresa Banks, and Cooper urges her not to accept. Annie Blackburn (Heather Graham), a character who arrives late in the run of the television series and develops a romantic relationship with Cooper, appears later in Laura's dream, after she has seemingly woken up and is lying in her bed, foreshadowing events from the series finale, as she tells Laura, 'My name is Annie. I've been with Dale and Laura. The good Dale is in the Lodge, and he can't leave. Write it in your diary.'

Secret sharers

Whether or not Laura records this dream is unknown, but what does eventually become established in the series is that several nights later Laura had a second, precognitive dream set in the Red Room, which she describes in her secret diary (Laura, a woman with two personalities – one secret, one public – keeps two diaries – one secret and one not – further illustrations of the duality so persistent in *Twin Peaks*). Cooper eventually comes across this diary entry during his investigation into Laura's death; it is dated 22 February, the night before the murder (although this day is within the time period covered in *Fire Walk With Me*, the film includes no references to the second dream). Donna Hayward (Lara Flynn Boyle) reads the entry aloud as Cooper and Deputy Andy Brennan (Harry Goaz) listen: 'Last night I had the strangest dream,' Donna recites, and as she proceeds to describe it, the camera closes in on Cooper's eye, dissolving to images of his own dream, and it soon becomes obvious that Laura is describing precisely the same dream that he himself had in *Twin Peaks*' episode 'Zen, or the Skill to Catch a Killer' (Season 1, Episode 3):

I was in a red room with a small man dressed in red and an old man sitting in a chair. I tried to talk to him. I wanted to tell him who BOB is, because I thought he could help me. My words came out slow and odd. It was frustrating trying to talk. I got up and walked to the old man. Then I leaned over and whispered the secret in his ear. Somebody has to stop BOB. BOB's only afraid of one man. He told me once. A man named MIKE. I wonder if this was MIKE in my dream. I hope he heard me. No one in the real world would believe me.

The old man in the dream is in fact not MIKE – BOB's one-time companion in terror, who has since 'seen the face of God' and repented – but rather an aged Cooper, and the secret that Laura whispers into his ear is the identity of her killer, whom she identifies as 'my father' – even though she is, at the time she is having this dream, still alive (while Laura imparts the same wisdom to Cooper in his own dream, he is unable to retain the

Bond on Bond: Laura Palmer and Agent Cooper in *Twin Peaks*
David Bushman

Fig. 3: Laura whispers a secret in elderly Dale Cooper's ear.

Fig. 4: Agent Cooper, Laura's paladin, protects her dignity in death.

information upon awakening, and thus the investigation goes on). The uncovering of this diary entry documents a profound bond between Laura and Cooper: not only did they dream the same dream, but Laura is pining here for the G-man to emerge as her paladin. This is a particularly meaningful development in light of Cooper's ultimate inability to prevent her tragic fate, evoking a defining moment from his past in which he failed to protect the love of his life, Caroline Earle, from death at the hands of her deranged husband Windom (Kenneth Walsh), himself an FBI agent and Cooper's one-time mentor. It also renders even more poignant a scene from the first season of the television series, in which Cooper – having just mediated a dispute between Albert Rosenfield, who was angling to conduct additional tests on Laura's corpse, and Doc Hayward (Warren Frost), who is seeking to prevent Albert from drilling a hole in Laura's head so that he can release the body for the funeral, by siding with the doctor – is left alone in the morgue with Laura and, noticing that her arm is dangling from the table, gently takes her discoloured hand and places it upon her chest: unable to guard her in life, he will at least protect her dignity in death.

Never believe it's not so

The discovery of this shared dream has a galvanizing effect on Cooper, who becomes even more convinced that his dream was a coded message, and that, as he himself had explained it to Sheriff Harry S. Truman (Michael Ontkean): 'Break the code, solve the crime.' After rounding up all of the suspects at the Roadhouse, a local watering hole, he tells the assembled:

As a member of the bureau, I spend most of my time seeking simple answers to difficult questions. In pursuit of Laura's killer, I have employed bureau guidelines, deductive technique, Tibetan method, instinct, and luck. But now I find myself in need of something new, which, for lack of a better word, we shall call 'magic.'

On cue, the room freezes, at which point Cooper begins to re-experience key moments from his dream – first the dancing dwarf, then Laura whispering the elusive words into his ear: 'My father killed me.' This then leads to the arrest of Leland Palmer, and the subsequent revelation that, possessed by BOB, he had repeatedly raped and eventually murdered his daughter.

This history of abuse, compounded by confirmation of Laura's suspicion that the perpetrator was her father (who typically came to her in the guise of BOB), obviously rendered Laura severely traumatized, a condition manifested by her cracked persona: on the one hand Laura was the paradigmatic 'good kid' – homecoming queen, Meals on Wheels volunteer, special-education and English-as-a-second-language tutor; on the other, she lived a deeply depraved double life involving drugs, promiscuity and sex for hire. (Lynch, in response to a question from Rodley about why he felt compelled to make *Twin Peaks: Fire Walk With Me* after the series was cancelled by ABC, responded: 'I couldn't get myself to leave the world of Twin Peaks. I was in love with the character of Laura Palmer and her contradictions: radiant on the surface but dying inside.')

As established earlier, Cooper, too, is emotionally battered by the death of Caroline Earle, as he suggests in the following exchange with Audrey Horne (Sherilyn Fenn), daughter of the exceedingly wealthy yet morally bankrupt business mogul Benjamin Horne (Richard Beymer), who carries a wicked crush on the G-man, and here is attempting to penetrate his aloofness:

Audrey: Someone must have hurt you really badly.
Cooper: No, someone was hurt by me, and I'll never let that happen again.
Audrey: What happened: did she die or something?
Cooper: Matter of fact, she did.

Whatever mystical forces are at play in forging the bond between Laura and Cooper, this shared history of emotional devastation must be viewed as at least equally responsible. It's worth noting that Laura and Cooper are both compulsive chroniclers of their own lives – Cooper through his trusty pocket tape recorder (addressing all of his comments – from the weather to the details of his culinary experiences, to his reverence for the town's towering Douglas firs – to the forever unseen Diane), and Laura through her diaries – with both seeking to impose some semblance of order on the chaos unfolding around them. For Cooper, this preoccupation with control extends even to his breakfast order – two eggs over easy, freshly-squeezed grapefruit juice, and bacon 'super crispy, almost burned, cremated.' For Laura, this impulse can be manifested, more maliciously, in an urge to manipulate people, as illustrated in this conversation between her psychiatrist, Dr. Lawrence Jacoby (Russ Tamblyn), and Bobby Briggs (Dana Ashbrook), her 'public' boyfriend:

Jacoby: Did you sometimes have the feeling that Laura was harbouring some awful secret?
Bobby: Yeah.
Jacoby: Bad enough that it drove her to consciously try to find people's weaknesses and prey on them, tempt them, break them down, make them do terrible, degrading things?'
Bobby: Yes.

Bond on Bond: Laura Palmer and Agent Cooper in *Twin Peaks*
David Bushman

Jacoby: Laura wanted to corrupt people because that's how she felt about herself?
Bobby: Yes.
Jacoby: Is that what happened to you, Bobby? Is that what Laura did to you?
Bobby (crying): She wanted so much. She made me sell drugs so she could have them.

'Truth-seeker'

Catherine Nickerson, in her 1993 essay 'Serial detection and serial killers in *Twin Peaks*', describes Cooper as an 'indefatigable truth seeker', likening him to Dashiell Hammett's Continental Op in *Red Harvest*, 'who continues investigating the goings-on in Poisonville even after his client fires him [...].' (In one scene, Sheriff Truman asks what he is getting at after intimating that Truman may not know all he needs to about his girlfriend, Josie Packard (Joan Chen), Cooper replies, 'The truth, Harry. That's my job.') Also like Hammett's Op, Cooper is a stranger in a strange land, thrust into an insular, iniquitous community drenched in secrets; his entire reason for being in Twin Peaks is to solve the über-mystery of who killed Laura Palmer, a town treasure, whose homecoming-queen photo is prominently displayed in the high school's trophy case. Cooper is forever poking around for answers, both small ('Sheriff, what kind of fantastic trees have you got growing up around here?') and large ('Is it any easier to believe a man would rape and murder his own daughter, any more comforting?' he asks after BOB is exposed as the malevolent spirit inhabiting Leland's body), antagonizing many of the town's denizens in the process – Josie, a woman with a sordid past of her own, even tries to gun him down in his hotel room, fearful of the secrets he'll uncover.

Detective fiction, Nickerson writes, 'has two sets of contradictory impulses', which she labels narratives of disclosure and concealment. Cooper, as sleuth, embodies the first, Laura the latter. This relationship is explicitly established early on, in Episode 6 of Season 1 ('Cooper's Dreams'), when Audrey Horne tells Cooper that 'Laura had a lot of secrets,' to which Cooper replies: 'Finding those out is my job.' Twin Peaks returns again and again to this shadow life of Laura's, as when Jacoby comments to Cooper and Truman that 'Laura had secrets, and around those secrets she built a fortress', or when Cooper, during his Red Room dream, engages in the following exchange with Laura and The Man from Another Place, suggesting that even Laura had lost track of who she really was after years of torment and abuse inflicted upon her by Leland/BOB:

Man from Another Place: She's my cousin. But doesn't she look almost exactly like Laura Palmer?
Cooper: But it – it is Laura Palmer. Are you Laura Palmer?
Laura: I feel like I know her, but sometimes my arms bend back.
Man from Another Place: She's filled with secrets.

Fig. 5: Clues left behind by
Laura.

There is, however, one person with whom Laura appears willing – even eager – to share those secrets: Agent Dale Cooper, a character she has never even met, other than in her dreams. Throughout *Twin Peaks*, Laura scatters hints like bread crumbs from beyond the grave to steer Cooper's investigation into what her life was really like, and who was responsible for ending it. In one scene, for example, Cooper, attempts to determine the identity of the person who possesses the other half of Laura's heart-shaped locket, and spots the reflection of James Hurley's (James Marshall) motorcycle in Laura's iris, while watching a home video of Laura and Donna Hayward picnicking. In another instance, Cooper and Truman discover a copy of *Flesh World* magazine in Laura's safety-deposit box, with a photo of Ronette Pulaski among the display ads. Ultimately, of course, the most significant of all the clues Laura leaves behind is the revelation, during the Red Room dream, that it was her father who murdered her.

Angels and demons

After his apprehension, as Leland lays dying in his jail cell, gripped by horror and remorse now that BOB has finally vacated his body, it is Cooper and Laura who together guide him toward his absolution – Cooper gently coaxing him verbally toward the 'light', Laura waiting there for him to bestow forgiveness:

> Cooper: Into the light, Leland, into the light.
> Leland: I see...her. She's...
> Cooper: Into the light, Leland.
> Leland: She's beautiful.
> Cooper: Into the light.
> Leland: Laura.

Fittingly, when the series *Twin Peaks* and the film *Twin Peaks: Fire Walk with Me* are viewed in the chronology in which they were made, the last images we see of Laura

Bond on Bond: Laura Palmer and Agent Cooper in *Twin Peaks*
David Bushman

*Fig. 6: Laura and Dale reunited in
the Red Room.*

Palmer are spectral; post-death, she is depicted sitting on a chair in the Red Room – Laura's death haunted not just 'each and every man, woman, and child' in Twin Peaks, as Cooper tells Albert Rosenfield, but also Lynch himself, and the multitudes of viewers who followed the show on television and are still following it on Internet sites and at fan conventions. Yet, perhaps no one's life was altered more by Laura's death than Cooper's, and it is the FBI agent who appears in the Red Room with Laura in this final scene, his hand resting gently on her back, as Laura – in all her stunning beauty – stares blissfully up at her hovering guardian angel, smiling, laughing, crying tears of joy, freed at last of her demons. ●

~~~~~~~~~~~~~~

GO FURTHER

Books

Lynch on Lynch
Chris Rodley
(London: Faber & Faber, 2005)

Chapter
9

Strange Spaces: Cult Topographies in *Twin Peaks*

Fran Pheasant-Kelly

→ The cult status of *Twin Peaks* (1990-91) is uncontested, evidenced by strong viewing figures, three Golden Globes and two Emmys, with various sources since rating the series as one of the greatest television shows of all time. Although *Twin Peaks* faltered in its second season, robust sales of the 20th anniversary DVD box set indicate its ongoing popularity. The anniversary also saw an inaugural UK 'Twin Peaks Festival', and a thirty-two hour continuous screening of all episodes at London Battersea Arts Centre that attracted 500 viewers and sold out in three hours. Numerous Internet user groups and weblogs further point to *Twin Peaks'* continued appeal with sites detailing viewers' responses to the series, and identifying locations with which it is associated.

Certainly, the term cult is usually understood through audience involvement, with academic scholarship endorsing this view. For example, in their essay *The Mainstream, Distinction and Cult TV* (2004), Mark Jancovich and Nathan Hunt contend that cult features are not intrinsic to the texts themselves, but emerge through fan responses. Janet Staiger expands on what exactly determines such responses in her 2000 book *Perverse Spectators*, explaining that cult engagement involves more intense displays of interest than seen in normal viewing activities. For Staiger, this includes expressing opinions, speculation, gossip and predictions, as well as a tendency to repeat memorized lines of dialogue. Surveys of fan websites clearly illustrate that *Twin Peaks* elicits such activities. Nonetheless, the privileging of audience over text in the elucidation of cult does not preclude a textual dimension. As Jancovich et al. further note in their 2003 book *Defining Cult Movies*, film-makers often share the same ideas and beliefs as fans, and so may set out to construct cult materials deliberately designed to appeal to certain viewers.

In this respect, Ernest Mathijs and Xavier Mendik's 2008 book *The Cult Film Reader* elaborates more closely upon the textual categories that distinguish cult: these include elements of innovation, transgression, badness, ambiguous generic identity, intertextuality, resistance to closure, nostalgia and gore. While *Twin Peaks* was a collaborative enterprise, these aspects invariably reflect Lynch's distinctive style. Typically, his work is weird, deviant or darkly comic. Unfamiliar characters, slow-motion cinematography and imagistic texture characterize his imagery, while narratives traverse genres and deal with difficult subjects ranging from incest to deformity. Additionally, his films often have surreal elements, unfolding in real or imaginary spaces that are ephemeral, nostalgic or concealed.

Twin Peaks evidently displays Lynch's hallmarks, promoting cult spectatorship through themes of incest and murder, generic indeterminacy, a vague evocation of the 1950s, intertexuality, lack of closure, and characters that extend from the nostalgically stylish to the grotesquely bizarre. Certainly, Twin Peaks' weird inhabitants, including the Log Lady, The Man from Another Place, and the One-Armed Man, are obvious sources of visual and narrative intrigue. For example, on one website, TV.com, fans describe *Twin Peaks'* individuals as 'consistently engaging', 'quirky' and 'weird, sexy, dirty and downright ugly'.

Yet, also essential to the cult following of *Twin Peaks* and further reflecting Lynch's influence, is its fascination with space, with one blog stating, 'the reasons that it is good [...] are One-Eyed Jacks and the Black Lodge'. Another comments on its 'strong, sometimes sickening colour schemes and the claustrophobic Red Room scenes like nothing seen on TV before'. For another fan, 'Lynch's second episode will be forever remembered for its disturbing, backwards talking dream sequence ending, with its red curtains

Strange Spaces: Cult Topographies in *Twin Peaks*
Fran Pheasant-Kelly

and dancing midget'.

In *Lynch on Lynch*, Lynch clarifies his preoccupation with space, discussing the unseen forces that underlie everyday existence. He suggests that close inspection not only reveals covert details, but may also render them abstract, explaining his attention to imagistic texture (as well as reflecting his artistic background). An appearance of normality overlying another traumatic world is therefore common to Lynchian visuals. In *Twin Peaks*, such trauma arises from Leland Palmer's possession by an evil spirit named BOB, who causes him to abuse his own daughter, Laura Palmer. Laura and Leland therefore inhabit an underworld that exists alongside their everyday lives, its transgressive and paranormal qualities providing cultish appeal.

Space in *Twin Peaks*

These two realms themselves comprise a highly differentiated array of spatialities, ranging from the Double R Diner through to the secret burial site of Laura Palmer's necklace seen in the pilot (Season 1, Episode 1). Some are microscopic, only visible under magnification, whilst others exist within the psychic spaces of dreams and hallucinations. Many are rendered strange through their apparent dislocation from time and space – for example, the series regularly features a traffic light suspended in mid air, swinging in the darkness, with repeated close-ups metaphorically important in mobilizing a sense of threat. Most obviously, the Red Room epitomizes Lynch's attention to otherworldly psychic spaces.

Another curiosity is the way that spatial conventions are inverted. The Great Northern Hotel exemplifies this tendency, animal trophies adorning its wooden interiors; while Leo and Shelley's home also seems unusual, their belongings located outdoors. Related to these visual idiosyncrasies is a consistent juxtaposition between natural and industrial spaces. The scene where Ronette Pulaski traverses a gigantic geometric structure at the sawmill set against a natural wild backdrop typifies this opposition; the binary implicitly reinforces Lynch's propensity to show two different worlds butting up against each other, their point of interface often being the site of menace or unpleasant event.

Moreover, the odd characteristics of these spaces correlate closely with the characters that frequent them, especially in connection to sound. Persistent distortions of sound, together with striking visual aspects, enhance the various spaces' cult potency. Most noticeable is the exaggerated sound of the wind blowing through the trees and the rushing sound of the waterfalls, both filmed in close-up and slow motion and appearing regularly throughout the series as if to signify a constant undercurrent of evil. Other examples include FBI Chief Gordon Cole's excessive shouting because of hearing difficulties, and an over-amplification of voices when Audrey is spying on her father from her hiding place in the Great Northern Hotel.

Fig. 1:
Audrey's secret passage in
the Great Northern Hotel.

In addition to sound distortion, lines of dialogue often seem puzzling, constantly inviting viewers to decipher their potential meaning. 'The owls are not what they seem,' a strange giant tells Agent Cooper, while the Log Lady reveals to him that 'my log saw something that night'. The opening scene of the pilot sees Pete Martell discover Laura's body lying on the beach, wrapped in plastic sheeting. He phones the sheriff to tell him, 'She's dead. Wrapped in plastic'. The term 'wrapped in plastic' thereafter became the title of a bimonthly fan magazine dedicated to stories about the series, which has been in publication since October 1992, and which appears on the first season's DVD special features. In general, the series' aesthetics combine with sound distortion, bizarre dialogue, and/or diegetic music to effect innovation.

'Real' spaces

The title itself, *Twin Peaks*, the name of the fictional town where the drama unfolds, signifies the centrality of location to the series. Its range of places includes various domestic spaces, whose *mise-en-scène* reflects their owners' eccentricities. Nadine and Ed Hurley's home is a typical example, camera close-ups of their living room mantelpiece revealing a collection of ornamental paraphernalia suggestive of Nadine's obsessive personality. Conversely, the Palmer's house features constant anguish and disjointed occurrences. In one scene, a distraught Leland dances with a photographic portrait of Laura, which he eventually drops and shatters. Sarah Palmer's sudden visions, rendered more frightening through rapid editing and melodramatic figure behaviour, are intrusive and visually jarring. Terrifying visions of BOB, who appears at the foot of Laura's bed or as Leland's reflected image, are also disturbing, slow motion and discontinuous editing heightening this effect. Extreme low-angle shots of the house's eerie stairwell and Maddie Ferguson's vision of a spreading bloodstain on the carpet further emphasize the uneasy atmosphere of the Palmer house.

Cult appeal especially derives from the town's public spaces, their memorable names including the Doubler R Diner, One-Eyed Jacks (a nearby casino and brothel), the Road-

Strange Spaces: Cult Topographies in *Twin Peaks*
Fran Pheasant-Kelly

Fig. 2: The Palmer house, menaced by the branches of an ominous dark tree.

———

Fig. 3: The Double R Diner.

house, The Bookhouse, Big Ed's Gas Farm and the Pink Room Disco. A focus for the television series is the Double R Diner, appearing in most episodes as a meeting place for either romantic liaisons or clandestine exchanges. It is mostly conjured as homely and nostalgic (though sometimes also strange and frightening), its 1950s' ambience mediated by a jukebox, red leather and chrome seating, and warm-toned colours and lighting. A seductive diegetic soundtrack (sound that is heard by the characters) invariably accompanies the interior shots. Importantly for cult audiences, and in line with Staiger's observation concerning memorized dialogue, the Double R Diner is connected to Agent Cooper's preoccupation with 'damn fine coffee and a slice of cherry pie'. In fact, this line of dialogue has become synonymous with the series, as indicated by website comments such as 'Twin Peaks boasts a terrific diner with a damn fine cup of coffee', while in *Lynch on Lynch*, Lynch notes how it achieved worldwide fame after *Twin Peaks*, with people going in to order cherry pie and coffee.

Also pivotal to the series' narrative is the nearby brothel, One-Eyed Jacks, owned by Benjamin Horne. Visually, One-Eyed Jacks comprises a *mise-en-scène* of scantily clad 'hostesses', whilst its voluminous curtains have a lurid, almost flesh-pink colour. A scene in which Horne disappears with one of the girls through a set of pink curtains draped to create the effect of entering a passageway therefore has distinctly erotic visual connotations.

More significantly, and contributing further to the series' theme of incest, Audrey Horne works there as a prostitute in order to uncover Laura's murderer. Here, she unwittingly encounters her father, who is unaware that the girl he is trying to seduce is his own daughter. The film version pursues sexual transgression and 'badness' in its equally explicit portrayal of the Pink Room Disco, a back room attached to the Roadhouse. In a lengthy sequence establishing the contexts for Laura's murder, the pulsing music, red-toned lighting and strobe lights create a hypnotic, sexually-charged atmosphere. Many of the girls are partially clad, and because the diegetic music drowns out any dialogue, the viewer (typically for Lynch) is coerced into a voyeuristic position. In fact, we have to watch intently to identify potential clues, and are thus engulfed in a dark Lynchian underworld, almost becoming accomplices in Laura's murder and decline into prostitution.

The Roadhouse too has cult possibilities in the mystifying reappearance of The Giant seen previously in Agent Cooper's dreams. In 'Demons' (Season 2, Episdoe 6), Cooper, Sheriff Truman and the Log Lady watch a chanteuse singing at the Roadhouse, when diegetic sounds seem to fade away, and a bright white spotlight replaces the garish orange-coloured lighting saturating the scene. From Cooper's point of view, we observe the singer seemingly disappear to be replaced by The Giant. As The Giant tells Cooper, 'it is happening again', Cooper's vision of him intercuts with the Palmer house, where Leland is looking at himself in the mirror to see BOB in reflection. The meaning of The Giant's words becomes clear as Leland/BOB subsequently attacks Laura's identical cousin, Maddy, the sequence unfolding in slow motion and accompanied by distorted screaming and growling sounds. Later, in resolving the name of the murderer, the series returns to the Roadhouse (Season 2, Episode 8, 'Drive with a Dead Girl'). Here, extreme canted camera angles, together with flashes of lightning, set a threatening tone for the revelation. Agent Cooper assembles potential suspects, including Leland, Ben, wheelchair-bound Leo and Bobby. Major Briggs and the Bellhop also turn up, and as the Bellhop says to Leland, 'that gum you like is going to come back in style' (another memorable line of dialogue), the scene freeze-frames, lightning flashes, and a moment of epiphany occurs for Cooper. He re-envisions the Red Room, and we can now hear Laura Palmer whisper to him 'my father killed me'.

Indeterminate spaces

Alongside these clearly delineated places exists a number of indeterminate spaces, including the realms of dreams, visions and even photographs that are conjured as real, physical worlds. In one example, we see Laura (who is asleep and obviously dreaming) enter a room that appears in a picture on her bedroom wall. However, we subsequently see her awake, looking at the same picture within which she is simultaneously visible, inferring crossover between conscious reality and unconscious fantasy.

The Red Room is also significant for fans, first appearing in one of Agent Cooper's dreams. The Red Room's potential for viewer fascination partly arises in its aesthetic incongruities, including its discordant arc deco furniture, Grecian-style statue and geometric design flooring, as well as the bizarre figure behaviour and dialogue of the characters in the room. These include a midget, dressed in red, an aged Agent Cooper, and Laura Palmer. On first sight, the midget, seen with his back turned to the viewer, shudders violently and involuntarily in an unnatural and protracted manner. An odd repetitive rustling sound accompanies the midget's action, and there is sound amplification as he then claps and rubs his hands together. An ensuing long shot reveals a shadow 'flying' across the red drapes, whilst Laura places her forefinger to her nose in a deliberate gesture that seems meaningful, yet leaves the viewer intrigued. 'She's filled with secrets,' the dwarf tells Cooper, another line of dialogue that too has assumed cult value. Predominantly, though, the Red Room's cult affect derives from the characters' odd-sounding dialogue (the characters speak backwards and then this is played in reverse), the strobing white light, and the sensuous jazzy music to which the dancing midget sways. Camerawork intensifies the scene's peculiarities – we first see the midget dance

Strange Spaces: Cult Topographies in *Twin Peaks*
Fran Pheasant-Kelly

Fig. 4:
The Red Room.

across the frame, a slow zoom-in framing him centrally, and then panning across the room to follow him, before it then pans slowly back to see Laura kiss Cooper and whisper in his ear. A cut to an overhead perspective of the dancing dwarf now discloses him more closely framed by the curtains as the closing credits come up.

Functioning differently in relation to cult is the murder site of Laura. Here, the surreal aesthetics and fluid camerawork of the Red Room are replaced by handheld camera. A panoramic shot sets the tone, mist drifting through the woods, before the camera cuts to the site of a disused rail carriage. Subjective camera from Cooper's perspective reveals the carriage's violent history, rendered compelling through flashlight-illuminated close-ups of bloodstains. Cooper and Truman come across one-half of a heart-shaped locket, raising questions about who possesses its other half. While maintaining the narrative's causal logic, it thus presents another enigma for fans. Close by is a torn piece of newsprint with the equally puzzling words, 'Fire walk with me', written in blood, of further import to the series' cult status.

In part, therefore, the series displays the generic iconography of the horror film, enhanced by frequent views of a full moon and its supernatural qualities. Episode two, 'Trace to Nowhere', sees Bobby and Mike meet with Leo Johnson in a drugs deal, where we witness them negotiating the woods by torchlight. Intercutting between long shot of the two enveloped in darkness and their point of view, our range of vision is limited to the circle illuminated by their torch. Here, as Bobby and Mike recover a hidden drug stash, another torch suddenly illuminates the scene, startling both characters and audience alike. A low-angle shot looks up towards Leo, torchlight under-lighting his face and adding to his menacing appearance, whilst in the background Bobby notices a silent black figure slip away into the darkness.

The recurrent visual reference to the wind blowing through the trees surrounding Twin Peaks further conveys an air of foreboding. Sheriff Truman confirms this association when he tells Agent Cooper, 'there's a sort of evil out there. There's something very, very strange in these old woods.' The woods are also the site where Cooper finally accesses the Red Room, located within the Black Lodge, which Hawk describes as a shadow of the White Lodge, where 'spirits that rule man and nature reside'. Cooper gains entry to the Black Lodge by standing within a circle of sycamore trees – a red curtain bizarrely materializes, through which he enters the Red Room and re-encounters the Bellhop, The Giant, the midget (The Man from Another Place) and both Laura Palmer and Maddy Ferguson, as well as his other self.

Additional to these psychic and liminal spaces, *Twin Peaks*' strangeness further emerges in its depictions of empty corridors and stairwells. For example, a school corridor is eerily vacant immediately after Laura's death, a static long shot of the empty corridor as we hear the headmaster announce her death conveying the sense of loss felt by her friends. An identical viewpoint of a corridor leading to the hospital room where

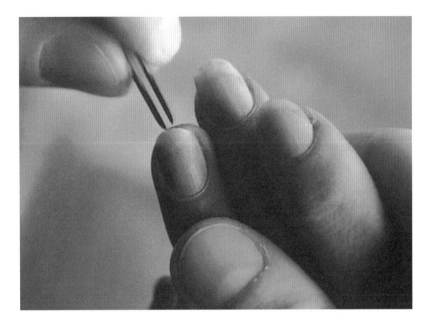

Fig. 5:
Laura's body – filled with secrets...

Ronette Pulaski lies in a coma is similarly disquieting. Here, a forward tracking shot through the corridor heightens its unsettling aspects. In both the film and series, recurring images of the stairwell in Laura's house are likewise ominous, with low camera angles consistently looking up towards the ceiling fan, and the repetitive whirring sound of its slow-motion rotation becomes both an indicator of, and metaphor for, Laura's rape by her father.

Another disturbing allusion to Laura's rape occurs at her funeral when a grief-stricken Leland throws himself into the grave on top of Laura's coffin, its faulty movement mechanism causing the coffin to rise up and down repeatedly. The camera position situates the viewer within the grave itself, such close proximity heightening its traumatic realness. At the same time, the amplified grating sound of the mechanism intrudes into the silence of the burial scene, causing it to become darkly humorous, particularly for Shelley when she recounts its comic effect to her customers afterwards at the Double R Diner.

Hidden and invisible spaces

Typical of Lynch's oeuvre, hidden spaces pervade *Twin Peaks* – for example, Audrey accesses a secret passage to spy on her father. Similarly, Josie Packard discovers the mill's ledgers in a safe hidden behind a bookcase panel while Catherine Martell conceals one of the ledgers in a compartment in her desk. Dr. Jacoby hides the heart locket in a coconut shell, whilst Shelley also has a secret place where she stores Leo's bloodstained shirt and a gun that she purchases to protect herself from him. Laura stows a tape in the top of a bedpost, while her second diary is discovered behind a book panel in Harold Smith's home.

Imagistic texture as hidden space repeatedly unfolds through image magnification, and consequently, there is a tendency for the camera to either cut to ultra close-up, or zoom in to extreme close-up. For example, Agent Cooper often uses a magnifying loupe to examine evidence, and in scrutinizing Laura's fingernail, we watch in close-up as he

Strange Spaces: Cult Topographies in *Twin Peaks*
Fran Pheasant-Kelly

extracts a letter 'R' from beneath it. This motif is repeated in the film, where we also observe in gruesome microscopic detail the entire removal of another victim's fingernail
(that of Teresa Banks) and the extraction of a letter 'T' from beneath it. Similarly, in the
pilot, an extreme close-up of Laura Palmer's eye in a video recording, afforded through
a diegetic zoom on a screen within the story, reveals the reflection of her secret lover,
James Hurley. This uncovering of minute hidden spaces thus mirrors the series' broader
spatial binary of a conscious surface reality and a darker, unconscious fantasy world.

Conclusion

The definition of cult is contested, some seeing it solely as a form of audience expression, whilst others consider it an interplay between audience and film-maker. Though
a joint collaboration, Lynch's auteur vision is epitomized in *Twin Peaks*, which, with its
transgressive plot, bizarre characters and nostalgic *mise-en-scène*, has established a
cult following, evident through websites, fan publications and DVD success 20 years
after its television screening. While the characters are enigmatic and trigger much discussion, there is considerable cult fan, critical and scholarly attention to the spaces of
Twin Peaks. Lynch himself expresses a fascination with the microscopic or hidden un-
derside of life. Often entailing surreal visuals, the representation of certain spaces is innovative in the use of sound and dialogue. Spaces may be homely and nostalgic, though
in others we witness extreme violence. *Twin Peaks* therefore possesses melodramatic
tendencies, but also has horror features, rendering it generically ambiguous. This essay suggests that the cult phenomenon of *Twin Peaks* thus derives in part from spatial representations that closely reflect characterization. Alongside the various spaces
are intertextual references that may further encourage cult engagement. For example,
Leland Palmer is described as 'The Third Man', Agent Cooper is called 'Gary Cooper',
whilst the milk used to drug Sarah Palmer recalls the scene of poisoned milk in Hitchcock's *Notorious* (1946).

A particular consequence of its spatial predilections is Kyle Maclachlan's later association with melodramatic suburban space in *Sex and the City* (1998–2004) and
Desperate Housewives (2004–12). Arguably, its surreal imaginary spatialities also antici-
pated a trend towards the representation of mental space as a real narrative dimension,
as well as influencing the increasing narrative complexity that has more recently dominated mind-puzzle films such as Scorsese's *Shutter Island* (2010) and Nolan's *Inception*
(2010). ●

GO FURTHER

Books

Authorship and the Films of David Lynch: Aesthetic Receptions in Contemporary Hollywood
Antony Todd
(London: I.B. Tauris, 2012)

The Film Paintings of David Lynch
Allister McTaggart
(Bristol & Chicago: Intellect, 2010)

David Lynch
Michael Chion
(Berkeley: University of California Press, 2007)

The Impossible David Lynch
Todd McGowan
(New York: Columbia University Press, 2007)

Lynch on Lynch
Chris Rodley (ed.)
(New York: Faber and Faber, 2005)

The Cinema of David Lynch: American Dreams, Nightmare Visions
Sheen Erica and Annette Davison
(London: Wallflower Press, 2004)

Serial Television: Big Drama on the Small Screen
Glen Creeber
(London & New York: Palgrave Macmillan, 2004)

Defining Cult Movies: The Cultural Politics of Oppositional Taste
Mark Jancovich, Antonio Lazaro Roboll, Julian Stringer and Andy Willis (eds)
(Manchester & New York: Manchester University Press, 2003)

Perverse Spectators: The Practices of Film Reception
Janet Staiger
(New York & London: New York University Press, 2000)

Strange Spaces: Cult Topographies in *Twin Peaks*
Fran Pheasant-Kelly

The Passion of David Lynch: Wild At Heart in Hollywood
Martha Nochimson
(Austin: University of Texas Press, 1997)

Television's Second Golden Age: From Hill Street Blues to ER
Robert Thompson
(New York: Syracuse University Press, 1996)

Full of Secrets: Critical Approaches to Twin Peaks
Lavery David (ed.)
(Detroit: Wayne State University Press, 1995)

Textual Poachers: Television and Participatory Culture
Henry Jenkins
(London & New York: Routledge, 1992)

A Cinema Without Walls: Movies and Culture After Vietnam
Timothy Corrigan
(London & New York; Routledge, 1991)

Extracts/Essays/Articles

'Members only: cult TV from margins to mainstream'
Sergio Angelini and Miles Booy
In Stacey Abbott (ed.). *The Cult TV Book* (London: I.B. Tauris, 2010), pp. 19–27.

'*Twin Peaks* – A case study'
Miles Booy
In Stacey Abbott (ed.). *The Cult TV Book* (London: I.B. Tauris, 2010), pp. 28–30.

'Observations on cult television'
Roberta Pearson
In Stacey Abbott (ed.). *The Cult TV Book* (London: I.B. Tauris, 2010), pp. 7–17.

'*Twin Peaks*: 20 years on this supernatural soap is celebrated'
Luke Lewis
In *The Guardian*, 22 October 2010.

'*Twin Peaks*: How Laura Palmer's death marked the rebirth of TV drama'

Andrew Antony
In *The Observer*, 21 March 2010.

'What is cult film?'
Ernest Mathijs and Xavier Mendik
In Ernest Mathijs and Xavier Mendik (eds). *The Cult Film Reader* (Maidenhead & New York: McGraw Hill, 2008), pp. 1–11.

'Cinematic meaning in the work of David Lynch: Revisiting *Twin Peaks: Fire Walk with Me*, *Lost Highway* and *Mulholland Drive*'
Michael Vass
In *CineAction* (67), 2005, pp. 12–25.

'*Twin Peaks*: David Lynch and the serial-thriller soap'
Linda Ruth Williams
In Michael Hammond and Lucy Mazdon (eds). *The Contemporary Television Series* (Edinburgh: Edinburgh University Press, 2005), pp.

'The mainstream, distinction and cult TV'
Mark Jancovich and Nathan Hunt
In Sara Gwenllian-Jones and Roberta Pearson (eds). *Cult Television* (Minneapolis: University of Minnesota Press, 2004), pp. 27–44.

'Dreaming and the cinema of David Lynch'
Kelly Bulkeley
In *Dreaming* (13: 1), 2003, pp. 49–60.

'Agent Cooper's errand in the wilderness: *Twin Peaks* and American mythology'
Michael Carroll
In *Literature Film Quarterly* (21: 4), 1993, pp. 287–95.

'*Twin Peaks* and the television gothic'
Lenora Ledwon
In *Literature Film Quarterly* (21: 4), 1993, pp. 260–70.

'The media business: "Twin Peaks" may provide a ratings edge for ABC'
Bill Carter
In the *New York Times*, 16 April 1990,
Available at: http://nyti.ms/ZhUwn6

Strange Spaces: Cult Topographies in *Twin Peaks*
Fran Pheasant-Kelly

Websites

'IMDB Awards for *Twin Peaks*', http://www.imdb.com/title/tt0098936/awards

'IMDB User Reviews for *Twin Peaks*', http://www.imdb.com/title/tt0098936/awards

'TV.com Twin Peaks', http://www.tv.com/shows/twin-peaks/reviews/2

Film and Television

Desperate Housewives, Marc Cherry, creator (US: ABC, 2004–12).
Inception, Christopher Nolan, dir. (UK/US: Warner Bros, 2010).
Shutter Island, Martin Scorsese, dir. (US: Paramount, 2010).
Sex and the City, Darren Star, creator (US: HBO, 1998–2004).
The Third Man, Carol Reed, dir. (UK/US: London Film Productions/ British Lion Film Corporation, 1949).
Notorious, Alfred Hitchcock, dir. (US: RKO Radio Pictures, 1946).

HARRY,
I'M GOING TO LET YOU IN
ON A LITTLE SECRET.
EVERY DAY, ONCE A DAY,
GIVE YOURSELF A PRESENT.
DON'T PLAN IT,
DON'T WAIT FOR IT,
JUST LET IT HAPPEN.
IT COULD BE A NEW SHIRT
AT THE MEN'S STORE,
A CATNAP IN YOUR OFFICE CHAIR
OR TWO CUPS OF GOOD HOT BLACK
COFFEE. LIKE THIS.

DALE COOPER
SEASON 1, EPISODE 6

Chapter
10

Gothic Daemon BOB

Chris Murray

→ With the arrest of Leland Palmer for the murder of his daughter Laura, Dale Cooper announces that 'The answer was right in front of me from the very beginning' (Season 2, Episode 8; 'Drive with a Dead Girl'). Cooper explains that a number of clues identified Leland as the killer BOB. Like Leland, The Man from Another Place danced in Cooper's vision. In accordance with descriptions of BOB, Leland's hair turned grey. In Cooper's synopsis, the case appears simple: bodily the murderer has been in plain sight all along.

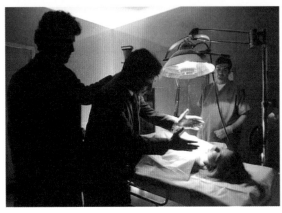

Fig. 1: BOB in Laura's bedroom.

———

Fig. 2: Leland's gesture, evocative of strangulation.

In fact, little that occurs in the town of Twin Peaks is truly a mystery. However, certain matters are made obscure because the society functions by the inhabitants' intentional disregard of unspeakable truths. The community reaches crisis because BOB accentuates and exposes its transgressive impulses, but he does not originate them. Charmed by Twin Peaks, Cooper embraces the town's mentality and overlooks a series of clues to BOB's identity. This wilful oblivion encourages BOB, who both personifies the dark side of the community and exploits the locals' reluctance to acknowledge its evils.

Even before the discovery of Laura Palmer's body, characters display uncanny knowledge of what has befallen the girl. When Sarah Palmer telephones Betty Briggs in search of Laura, she muses ominously, 'I'm wondering if maybe she went out with Leland' (Season 1, Episode 1; 'Northwest Passage'). Subsequently, Leland betrays his guilt in a number of scenes that represent BOB's flirtation with discovery. When Harry Truman approaches him in the Great Northern Hotel, Leland needs no explanation for the visit. Benjamin Horne asks what has happened, and without Harry's information, Leland answers, 'My daughter is dead.' When Leland sees Laura's corpse on the autopsy table, he reaches towards her, but not in caress. His thumb and fingers stretch apart in a gesture evocative of strangulation. It is the hand gesture that Albert Rosenfield mimics when he indicates how the killer cradled the dead Laura's chin to lift her head for a final kiss (Season 1, Episode 3; 'Zen, or the Skill to Catch a Killer').

As Leland breaks the frame that contains Laura's photo, he smears blood on the picture, and so recreates his last vision of his daughter alive (Season 1, Episode 2; 'Traces to Nowhere'). Amidst the arguments and breakdowns that travesty Laura's funeral, Leland straddles the coffin – which locked in mechanical malfunction rises and falls suggestively – and so provides a clue to the true nature of the relationship between father and daughter (Season 1, Episode 3). With such behaviour, BOB flaunts the truth, but people do not wish to see. The consequences of ignoring such information are clarified later in the series, when Maddy Ferguson anticipates her own imminent murder. In a vision of blood spreading across the carpet, she realizes that the Palmer household is a place of violence and death (Season 1, Episode 8; 'The Last Evening'). Typically of behaviour

Gothic Daemon BOB
Chris Murray

within the Twin Peaks community, Maddy suppresses this knowledge, which should impel her to flee to safety. She declines to analyze and act upon what she has seen, and dies consequently.

The murders perpetrated by Leland/BOB exemplify and exaggerate acts of crime and concealment in Twin Peaks, whose inhabitants lead double lives. This duplicity is not facilitated by ingeniously secretive behaviour, but apparently by tacit agreement not to recognize each other's vices. Hence some of the locals' secrets are obvious to the outsider, the inward-bound protagonist Dale Cooper, who perceives immediately that Harry is in love with the recent widow Josie Packard (Season 1, Episode 1), as Ed Hurley is involved with the married Norma Jennings (Season 1, Episode 3). Other truths are unbearable, and take longer to unearth. Addressing this reluctance, Cooper and Truman reflect on the credibility of BOB's existence, juxtaposed with the material facts of the Palmer murder. Cooper asks, 'Is it easier to believe that a man would rape and murder his own daughter?' (Season 2, Episode 16).

The repressions of Twin Peaks' inhabitants revive a persistent theme of American Gothic. The genre is haunted by buried histories, be they national, as in the Civil War origins of Washington Irving's Hessian horseman in *The Legend of Sleepy Hollow*, or personal, as Edgar Allan Poe explores in the enigmatic family of Usher, with its intimations of corruption and incest. The American idyll requires disavowal of the violent episodes in the country's history, a type of denial that is doubled by the personal secrets that characters harbour in American Gothic. David Lynch and Mark Frost allude to the national context in Ben Horne's Civil War fantasies, the peripheral presence of the Native American, Hawk, and the land-grabbing antics of Catherine Martell. Individually, everyone in Twin Peaks seems to conceal something, from the furtive military work of the virtuous Garland Briggs to the drug deals and prostitution that affected Laura and involve numerous other characters. The gothic genre explores the uncanny, Freud's *umheimlich*, which he defines in his 1919 essay as 'that class of the terrifying which leads back to something long known to us, once familiar [...] that ought to have to have remained hidden and secret, yet comes to light' (1948: 369–70). Attempts to suppress unpalatable truths are doomed; these matters will surface involuntarily in conscious thought in the form of strange occurrences which may seem supernatural. *Twin Peaks* is a gradual exposition of a community's secrets. Within this process of revelation, BOB functions as a catalyst. BOB impels Leland to commit the greatest crimes in *Twin Peaks*, to rape and murder his daughter, and subsequently the community begins to unearth its hidden corruption.

Gradually Cooper apprehends that BOB is a supernatural being who has possessed Leland, compelling him to kill Teresa Banks, Laura, Jacques Renault and Maddy. He understands also that BOB may inhabit and control other people. BOB is man, spirit and nature, associated with a disturbing human form – the alternate realm of the Black Lodge – and the owls that survey the nearby woods. As Philip Gerard/MIKE explains that he is 'similar to BOB', he claims that he is 'an inhabiting spirit', and the Gerard is a 'host' (Season 2, Episode 6; 'Demons'). When Leland is arrested, BOB acknowledges him as merely a 'vehicle' (Season 2, Episode 8). Leland recalls BOB's original act of possession: 'He went inside me […]. He made me do things, terrible things.' In Chris Rodley's collection of interviews, *Lynch on Lynch*, David Lynch describes BOB as 'an abstraction with a human form. That's not a new thing, but it's what BOB was' (2005: 180).

In his article 'Agent Cooper's errand in the wilderness,' Michael Carroll places *Twin Peaks* in a quintessentially American mythology, but he also likens Cooper to Odysseus, Aeneas and Dante as adventurers through 'the land of the dead' (1993: 288). Within Carroll's schematic, Hades is also a dualistic concept, both classical and American. Cooper follows his mythical predecessors literally when he journeys to the Black Lodge – a kind of afterlife – to encounter the deceased Laura, Leland, Maddy and Caroline. Yet he explores figurative American underworlds of crime and vice also. Comparably, BOB is a being of two universes. BOB's physicality, to those who can truly perceive it, assumes fearful tropes of American culture. His grizzled appearance – long-haired, unshaven in worn denim – evokes bikers and deadbeats. BOB might drink at the Roadhouse, associate with Leo Johnson and Hank Jennings, or smuggle drugs across the border. BOB's presence brings the smell of scorched engine oil, a stimulus both hellish and quotidian. However, as an entity – an unseen, possessive spirit – BOB resembles the daemon of classical literature. In Plato's *Symposium*, Diotima refers to 'many and various' daemonic spirits that 'shuttle back and forth' between gods and humans: 'Gods do not mix with men; they mingle and converse with us through spirits instead' (1997: 486). Likewise in the 'Fire Walk with Me' poem that recurs in *Twin Peaks*, BOB exists 'between two worlds,' this world and the Black Lodge. I suggest a particular parallel with Greek tragedy, in which the daemon possesses a character and impels decisive actions. For example, in Euripides' play *Heracles*, the hero slays his children. In Sophocles' *King Oedipus*, when the hero puts out his eyes at the discovery of Jocasta's body, the Chorus assumes that a daemon must have moved him. As in *King Oedipus*, the murder and incest committed by BOB/Leland entails daemonic possession and confused identity. In ignorance, Oedipus kills his father and marries his mother. Leland is driven to abuse and kills his daughter, but appears not to realize it until he nears death (Season 2, Episode 8). Laura, by BOB's power to beguile perception, is slow to comprehend that her sex partner is her father. In both narratives, the fatal climax of the sexual relationship is consequential to the identification of the characters involved. Oedipus is no longer a heroic newcomer to Corinth, but a returned exile who participates in a love triangle, Oedipus-Jocasta-Laius, in which he has killed his rival, also his father. The BOB-Laura-Leland triangle ends in death because Laura gains knowledge of BOB's 'vehicle'. Given Freud's psychological interpretations of the Oedipus myth, we might also speculate that BOB identifies and encourages an incestuous impulse that already exists in Leland, rather than manipulating him into acts and thoughts that are entirely alien to him.

To compare *Twin Peaks* to tragedy entails the question of whether Leland has committed *hamartia*, some tragic error that provokes BOB or justifies his possession. It befits American Gothic's preoccupation with obscured evil that Leland first encountered BOB

Gothic Daemon BOB
Chris Murray

Fig. 3: BOB's reflection in mirrors.

Fig. 4: 'The answer was right in front of me from the very beginning' (Dale Cooper).

in the idyll of a wholesome, lakeside holiday. As the dying Leland recalls, BOB flicked matches at him and asked, 'Do you want to play with fire, little boy?' (Season 2, Episode 8). Young Leland was either tempted by the strange offer or unable to resist BOB's invasive spirit; in neither case does the child seem culpable for the catastrophe that follows. BOB claims that in adulthood Leland has 'a hole where his conscience used to be.' Professionally Leland is the great scourge of American society, an attorney. He is capable of ruthlessness, as in his cynical advice to Ben Horne on how to be rid of the Icelandic investors (Season 2, Episode 5; 'The Orchid's Curse'). Yet it is Leland's normality that appeals to BOB, who delights in the destruction of everyday life and relationships. He alludes to this with his choice of the all-American names 'BOB' and 'Robertson'. In the most banal places we see BOB reflected in mirrors: in living-rooms, family hallways and cars.

BOB wishes to bring low a businessman and a family figure, and revels in the domestic setting of the Palmer household. Hence Leland/BOB discusses a dinner date *hamartiahklmk*with Sarah as he takes up a golf bag containing Maddy's body, and exits with a hackneyed 'Bye, Hon' (Season 2, Episode 7; 'Lonely Souls').

Systematically, BOB dismantles Leland's life by tainting conventional activities. Under BOB's compulsion, Leland listens to old records in preparation for murder, swings recklessly back and forth across the road as he drives, and breaks down in social gatherings. Finally, having inflicted a fatal injury on Leland, BOB desolates him with realization of what he has been compelled to do.

BOB resembles the tragic daemon not only in his spiritual and causative traits, but in his evocation of tragedy's social function. Ultimately tragedy is purgative. The protagonist is a scapegoat who endures torment, and the catharsis that follows his/her misfortune benefits the wider community within the drama and, vicariously, the audience. In *King Oedipus* it is not only the ruler who is at fault: the people of Corinth have become irreligious and have lost faith in prophecy. Belief in the gods is restored by the ordeal of Oedipus, which is a kind of sacrifice. Cancelled by the television network, *Twin Peaks* ceases at a point where it is difficult to envision movement towards resolution, to peace in the town. Yet while BOB's social function is difficult to identify, he is strongly emblematic of the community's sin and repression, and puts Leland to sacrifice in ridicule of the hypocrisy in Twin Peaks.

Two characters' reflections on Laura's death seem hopelessly vague, yet hint unintentionally at BOB's true nature. Harry Truman refers to 'a sort of *evil* out there. Something very, very strange in these old *woods*' (Season 1, Episode 3). Albert Rosenfield muses that 'Maybe that's all BOB is. The evil that men do. Maybe it doesn't matter what we call it' (Season 2, Episode 16). These are attempts to relegate the evil behind Laura's death to distance, either figuratively, by denying BOB's literalness, or spatially, by associating him with the woods outside the town. Yet BOB is within Twin Peaks, and BOB *is* Twin Peaks. The old evil is of the town as well as outside it, exemplified by BOB's inhabitation of a man whose ancestry, his neighbours suggest, makes him synonymous with Twin Peaks. When Leland is charged for the murder of Jacques Renault, Harry argues that he should be granted bail on the grounds that 'his roots go way back. His grandfather, Joshua Palmer, brought the family here more than 75 years ago' (Season 2, Episode 4; 'Laura's Secret Diary'). Oldness is evil; oldness is good. Harry does not see that both are manifest within the same pillar of the community's heritage. When he kills Laura, BOB initiates an escalation and revelation of secretive activities in the town: the mill is burned, Cooper and Leo Johnson are shot, Bobby Briggs frames James Hurley, Nadine Hurley attempts suicide, and Windom Earle gravitates towards the region's inherent powers of evil. Sightings of BOB increase with this deepening crisis. In this context, investigators are slow to suspect that Leland is Laura's murderer, and the case is complicated because so many characters are readily identifiable with the pathological behaviour of BOB.

While the facts of Laura's last days are established in painstaking detail by Cooper's investigation, the prequel *Fire Walk with Me* (Lynch, 1992) returns to narrate those events explicitly. The focus narrows to the incestuous love triangle and Laura's desperation as she nears death. Pathetically she attempts to persuade herself that 'it can't be him'. In tense scenes, the Palmers allude to the terrible half-knowledge they possess. The family dynamic, perverted by BOB's agency, is apparent to each of them; they approach it but are unable to confront it. As the family sits down to dinner, Sarah Palmer is unsettled by the terms in which Leland questions Laura over her necklace: 'Did you get this from your lover?' he asks, handling the necklace; 'They don't call them lovers in high school, Leland,' Sarah insists. As a parent she wishes to deny her daughter's sexual activity, but more strongly to disavow her husband's improper knowledge of, and intrusion into, Laura's sex life. Sarah has had a vision of a white horse – a symbol of chastity and innocence – but it appeared only momentarily, only to vanish. It was a mythical impossibility, a signifier that does not represent the Palmer household. As the kitchen scene continues, Leland begins to pinch Laura's cheeks. His playfulness is sexual rather than paternal. Sarah protests: 'Don't do that. She doesn't like it.' Cruelly, Leland rebuffs, 'How do you know what she doesn't like?' He is blunt, clarifying Sarah's exclusion from his relationship with Laura, and he makes obvious his forbidden knowledge of what, physically, his daughter 'likes'. Sarah shrieks, 'Stop it!' BOB manipulates the Palmers to hysteria with these games, and they find the implications unbearable: they drop the sub-

Gothic Daemon BOB
Chris Murray

*Fig. 5: 'How do you know what she
doesn't like?' (BOB/Leland).*

*Fig. 6: 'It's him! It's your father!'
(MIKE).*

ject immediately, and resume domestic roles. Sarah tells
Leland to sit, Leland tells Laura to wash her hands, Sarah
puts dinner on the table.

The emotional pitch of the dinner scene returns when
Gerard/MIKE confronts BOB/Leland at a traffic light. MIKE
shouts to Laura, 'It's him! It's your father!' Leland revs the
engine to drown out MIKE's voice, but by doing so provides
Laura with another clue to BOB's identity, the stench of
burnt engine oil. Still Laura refuses to see the truth but,
because it is almost undeniable now, she is badly troubled
by the encounter.

The dramatic climax of the film follows, not with Laura's death – which is inevitable – but in the scene of tragic
recognition. BOB prowls into Laura's bed. After a few moments, she sees that BOB is
her father, and screams. Later, by BOB's malevolent ventriloquism, Leland speaks with
the tone of someone who has offended unintentionally: 'I always thought you knew it
was me.' BOB insists that Laura has known his human identity and participated willingly
in their relationship. In the mirror, Laura sees a vision of herself as BOB. While she has
resisted his direct spiritual possession of her, she has prostituted herself and associated
with lowlifes; she has succumbed to the evil that BOB personifies.

At Laura's funeral, Bobby Briggs confronts his neighbours with their collective re-
sponsibility for his girlfriend's death. Bobby understands the corruption of Twin Peaks
well. The power of Twin Peaks – of its evil atmosphere – to degrade its inhabitants parallels BOB's spiritual possession of Leland. As the series progresses we perceive in Bobby a sophisticated form of character development in retrospect. We understand that
events prior to the beginning of the series have prompted him to change abruptly into a
drug dealer and a thug. Jacoby reveals that Laura laughed at Bobby's first sexual performance (Season 1, Episode 5; 'The One-Armed Man'). Hurt by this, Bobby opened himself
to experiences that would harden him into the deviant we encounter in the series. He
was exposed like the young Leland meeting the enigmatic BOB. While Bobby does not
guess at the existence of BOB, he knows that the town is conducive to evil. The anguish
of Bobby's funeral tirade lies in his perception that atrocities like Laura's death, which
express the concealed spirit of Twin Peaks, are preventable:

What are you waiting for? You make me sick. Damn hypocrites, you make me sick!
Everybody knew she was in trouble, but we didn't do anything. All you good people. You
wanna know who killed Laura? You did! We all did! (Season 1, Episode 3)

Tom O'Connor, in his article on 'Bourgeois myth versus media poetry' in *Twin Peaks*,
discusses the locals' denial of their communal guilt for the murder. To O'Connor, because of the 'private' nature of the 'sexualized murder', Laura's death is '"haemorrhaged"
by social authority to the realm of personal fantasy' (2004: 317). Silently, the locals seize

on the sordid details of Laura's murder to dismiss it to the realm of the unspeakable. They will only acknowledge the civic necessity that the killer should be apprehended and punished formally by the authorities. They will not recognize that collectively they create an environment in which terrible violence occurs, and that Laura's murder is the synecdoche of a pervasive evil. This suppression is itself a forceful, psychologically violent act – as O'Connor suggests with the gruesome 'haemorrhage' metaphor – that doubles BOB's murder of Laura because of her knowledge. The inhabitants of Twin Peaks create a home for BOB with their vice, and their silence is licence for him to do as he wishes. Bobby shouts, 'Everybody knew.' BOB/Leland lies on top of the dead Laura. The townsfolk turn away. ●

GO FURTHER

Books
Plato: Complete Works
John M. Cooper (ed.)
(Indiana: Hackett Publishing Company, 1997)

The Three Theban Plays: Antigone, Oedipus the King, Oedipus at Colonus
Sophocles (trans. Robert Fagles)
(London: Allen Lane, 1982)

Extracts/Essays/Articles
'Bourgeois myth versus media poetry: Re-visiting Mark Frost and David Lynch's *Twin Peaks*'
Tom O'Connor
In *Social Semiotics* (14: 3), 2004, pp. 309-33.

'Agent Cooper's errand in the wilderness: *Twin Peaks* and American mythology'
Michael Carroll
In *Literature / Film Quarterly* (21: 4), 1993, pp. 287-94.

'*Twin Peaks*: Rewriting the sensation novel'
Melynda Huskey
In *Literature/Film Quarterly* (21: 4), 1993, pp. 248-54.

'The Uncanny'
Sigmund Freud
In *Collected Papers Volume IV* (London: Hogarth Press, 1948), pp. 368-407.

Going Further

Books

Authorship and the Films of David Lynch: Aesthetic Receptions in Contemporary Hollywood
Antony Todd
(London: I.B. Tauris, 2012)

The Film Paintings of David Lynch
Allister McTaggart
(Bristol & Chicago: Intellect, 2010)

Dreaming in the World's Religions: A Comparative History
Kelly Bulkeley
(New York: New York University Press, 2008)

David Lynch
Michael Chion
(Berkeley: University of California Press, 2007)

The Impossible David Lynch
Todd McGowan
(New York: Columbia University Press, 2007)

Lynch on Lynch
Chris Rodley (ed.)
(New York: Faber and Faber, 2005)

The Cinema of David Lynch: American Dreams, Nightmare Visions
Sheen Erica and Annette Davison
(London: Wallflower Press, 2004)

Serial Television: Big Drama on the Small Screen
Glen Creeber
(London & New York: Palgrave Macmillan, 2004)

Defining Cult Movies: The Cultural Politics of Oppositional Taste
Mark Jancovich, Antonio Lazaro Reboll, Julian Stringer and Andy Willis (eds)
(Manchester & New York: Manchester University Press, 2003)

Perverse Spectators: The Practices of Film Reception

Janet Staiger
(New York & London: New York University Press, 2000)

Plato: Complete Works
John M. Cooper (ed.)
(Indiana: Hackett Publishing Company, 1997)

The Passion of David Lynch: Wild At Heart in Hollywood
Martha Nochimson
(Austin: University of Texas Press, 1997)

Television's Second Golden Age: From Hill Street Blues to ER
Robert Thompson
(New York: Syracuse University Press, 1996)

Full of Secrets: Critical Approaches to Twin Peaks
Lavery David (ed.)
(Detroit: Wayne State University Press, 1995)

Textual Poachers: Television and Participatory Culture
Henry Jenkins
(London & New York: Routledge, 1992)

A Cinema Without Walls: Movies and Culture After Vietnam
Timothy Corrigan
(London & New York; Routledge, 1991)

Twin Peaks: An Access Guide
David Lynch
(Berkeley: University of California Press, 1991)

The Autobiography of F.B.I. Special Agent Dale Cooper. My Life, My Tapes
Scott Frost
(New York: Pocket, 1991)

The Secret Diary of Laura Palmer
Jennifer Lynch
(New York: Pocket, 1990)

The Three Theban Plays: Antigone, Oedipus the King, Oedipus at Colonus

Sophocles (trans. Robert Fagles)
(London: Allen Lane, 1982)
The Ritual Process: Structure and Anti-Structure
Victor Turner
(Piscataway, NJ: Aldine Transaction, [1969] 1995)

The Rites of Passage
Arnold Van Gennep
Chicago: University of Chicago Press, [1909] 1960)

Extracts/Essays/Articles

'The significant event: Establishing universes, creating movements'
Gry Worre Hallberg
In *House of Futures* (issue 2), April 2012.

'Members only: Cult TV from margins to mainstream'
Sergio Angelini and Miles Booy
In Stacey Abbott (ed.). *The Cult TV Book* (London: I.B. Tauris, 2010), pp. 19–27.

'*Twin Peaks* – A case study'
Miles Booy
In Stacey Abbott (ed.). *The Cult TV Book* (London: I.B. Tauris, 2010), pp. 28–30.

'Observations on cult television'
Roberta Pearson
In Stacey Abbott (ed.). *The Cult TV Book* (London: I.B. Tauris, 2010), pp. 7–17.

'*Twin Peaks*: 20 years on this supernatural soap is celebrated'
 Luke Lewis
In *The Guardian*, 22 October, 2010.

'*Twin Peaks*: How Laura Palmer's death marked the rebirth of TV drama'
Andrew Antony
In *The Observer*, 21 March 2010.

'*Twin Peaks: Fire Walk with Me*: The Press Conference at Cannes 1992'
S. Murray
In Barney A. Richard (ed.). *David Lynch – Interviews* (The University of Mississippi Press, 2009).

'What is cult film?'
Ernest Mathijs and Xavier Mendik
In Ernest Mathijs and Xavier Mendik (eds). *The Cult Film Reader* (Maidenhead & New York: McGraw Hill, 2008), pp. 1–11.

'Cinematic meaning in the work of David Lynch: Revisiting *Twin Peaks Fire Walk with Me*, *Lost Highway* and *Mulholland Drive*'
Michael Vass
In *Cinem'Action* (67), 2005, pp.12–25.

'*Twin Peaks*: David Lynch and the serial-thriller soap'
Linda Ruth Williams
In Michael Hammond and Lucy Mazdon (eds). *The Contemporary Television Series* (Edinburgh: Edinburgh University Press, 2005)

'The mainstream, distinction and cult TV'
Mark Jancovich and Nathan Hunt
In Sara Gwenllian-Jones and Roberta Pearson (eds). *Cult Television* (Minneapolis: University of Minnesota Press, 2004), pp. 27–44.

'Bourgeois myth versus media poetry: Re-visiting Mark Frost and David Lynch's *Twin Peaks*'
Tom O'Connor
In *Social Semiotics* (14: 3), 2004, pp. 309–33.

'Dreaming and the cinema of David Lynch'
Kelly Bulkeley
In *Dreaming* (13: 1), 2003, pp. 49–60.

'Gender, power and culture in the televisual world of *Twin Peaks*: A feminist critique'
Sue Lafky
In *Journal of Film and Video* (51), 2000, pp. 5–19.

'Lynching women'
Diana Hume George
In David Lavery (ed.) *Full of Secrets: Critical Approaches to Twin Peaks* (Detroit: Wayne State University Press, 1995)

'*Twin Peaks* and the television gothic'

Lenora Ledwon
In *Literature Film Quarterly* (21: 4), 1993, pp. 260–70.

'Agent Cooper's errand in the wilderness: *Twin Peaks* and American mythology'
Michael Carroll
In *Literature Film Quarterly* (21: 4), 1993, pp. 287–95.

'*Twin Peaks*: Rewriting the sensation novel'
Melynda Huskey
In *Literature/Film Quarterly* (21: 4), 1993, pp. 248–54.

'Serial detection and serial killers in *Twin Peaks*'
Catherine Nickerson
In *Literature/Film Quarterly* (21: 4), 1993.

'The media business: *Twin Peaks* may provide a ratings edge for ABC'
Bill Carter
In *The New York Times*, 16 April 1990.

'The Uncanny'
Sigmund Freud
In Collected Papers Volume IV (London: Hogarth Press, 1948), pp. 368–407.

Websites

'Welcome to Twin Peaks', www.welcometotwinpeaks.com

'Black Lodge 2600 Game', http://jack.worlord.com/blacklodge2600/

'Twin Peaks Festival', http://twinpeaksfest.com/

'Twin Peaks UK Festival', www.twinpeaksukfestival.com/

'Sleep and Dream Database', http://sleepanddreamdatabase.org/

'Idiot Box Artwork', www.idiotbox88.blogspot.com/

'Never Before Seen *Twin Peaks* Photos', www.wired.com/underwire/2010/08/twin-peaks

'The Laura Palmer Doll Is Back!', www.jeremyriad.com/blog/toy-talk/the-laura-palmer-doll-is-back/

'Twin Peaks Agent Dale Cooper Custom Action Figure', www.figurerealm.com/ view-customfigure.php?FID=26746

'IMDB Awards for *Twin Peaks*', www.imdb.com/title/tt0098936/awards

'TV.com Twin Peaks', www.tv.com/shows/twin-peaks/reviews/2

'She's Full of Secrets', www.thestylerookie.com/2011/04/shes-full-of-secrets.html

'Twinpeaks4eva', www.Twinpeaks4eva.tumblr.com

"Twin Twin Peaks', www.**twintwinpeaks**.com

Film and Television

Desperate Housewives, Marc Cherry, creator (US: ABC, 2004–12).
Inception, Christopher Nolan, dir. (UK/US: Warner Bros, 2010).
Shutter Island, Martin Scorsese, dir. (US: Paramount, 2010).
Sex and the City, Darren Star, creator (US: HBO, 1998–2004).
The Third Man, Carol Reed, dir. (UK/US: London Film Productions/ British Lion Film Corporation, 1949).
Notorious, Alfred Hitchcock, dir. (US: RKO Radio Pictures, 1946).

Image Credits

From Twin Peaks the series
Intro: Fig. 1 p.5
Chapter 2: Figs 3-5 pages 23-24 & 26
Chapter 3: Fig. 6 p.38
Chapter 6: Figs 1-5 pages 68-72
Chapter 7: Figs 1-3 pages 78-79
Chapter 8: Fig. 1 p.86
            Fig.s 3-5 pages 88 & 91
Chapter 9: Fig. 1 page 97
            Figs 2-3 p. 98
            Fig. 5 p.101
Chapter 10: Fig. 2 p.109
            Figs 3-4 p. 112 ©Paramount Pictures

From Twin Peaks: Fire Walk With Me
Chapter 5: Figs 1-6 pages 56-60
Fan Appreciation 3: Figs 2-3 pages 64-65
Chapter 6: Fig. 6 p.73
Chapter 8: Fig. 2 p.87
            Fig. 6 p.92
Chapter 9: Fig. 4 p.100
Chapter 10: Fig. 1 p.109
            Figs 5-6 p.114 ©Warner Bros.

Additional Images

Chapter 1:   Figs 2 & 3 p.10 & 12 ©Twentieth Century Fox
                Fig. 4 p.13 ©Pacific Mountain Productions
                Fig. 5 p. 14 ©Fox Television Studios
                Fig. 6 p. 15 ©Jak Locke
Fan Appreciation 1: Fig. 1 p.16 & Fig.s 2 & 3 p.18 ©Shara Lorea Clarke
Chapter 2:   Fig. 1 p.21 ©Pin Interest
                Fig. 2 p.22 ©Etsy
                Fig. 13 p.28 ©Angela K Bayout
Chapter 3:   fig 1 p.33 ©Eric Goldmann
                Figs 2-3 p.24 ©Georgia Coffee
                Fig. 4 p.35 ©Inga Gerner Nielsen/Fiction Pimps
                Fig. 5 p. 37 ©Julie Johansen
Chapter 4:   Fig 1 p.41 ©Dudebox
                Fig. 2 p.42 ©ebay
                Fig. 3 p.42 ©Oz Sticker
                Fig. 4 p.43 ©Andrew Howe
                Fig. 5 p. 43 ©Kiersten Esserpreis
                Fig. 6 p.44 ©Brian Lens
Fan Appreciation 2: Pieter Dom Figs 1 & 2 p.50 & 52 ©Pieter Dom
Fan Appreciation 3: Fig. 1 p.62 ©National Museum of Singapore
Chapter 7:   Figs 4-5 pages 80 & 81 ©David Griffith

Contributor Details

EDITORS

Marisa C. Hayes (co-editor) is an interdisciplinary artist and scholar. Her first career in the performing arts led to cinema studies focused on dance films, as well as movement analysis in screen-based media. She is currently writing a doctoral thesis on body representation in film at the University of Paris, and was recently named Cultural Ambassador to Hong Kong by the regional government of Burgundy. Her French and English language publications include a variety of book essays and journal articles that explore the intersections of image-making (film & new media), the performing arts and literature. Marisa enjoys lounging with her cats and husband Franck (co-editor of this book) while watching everything from *giallo* (Italian horror) to early surrealist films, as well as her beloved *Buffy* and countless other series. She continues to dream that one day the Log Lady will have something to tell her.

Franck Boulègue (co-editor) has been passionate about *Twin Peaks* since its original broadcast and remembers 1992 as the year he was ostracized for his appreciation of the film. Originally from Lyon, France, Franck earned a degree in political science and communication from the Institut d'Etudes Politiques, and completed graduate studies in communication at the University of Liverpool. He is a regular contributor to *Eclipses*, a French film research journal for which he has analyzed the filmography of Tim Burton, Chris Marker and the Coen brothers, among others. His writing has also appeared in *Les Cahiers du Cinéma*'s book on Gus Van Sant (2009). His forthcoming publications include an essay on gender analysis for the book *Planet of the Apes and Philosophy* (Open Court, 2013), a text on Busby Berkley for the French film journal *Trafic*, and an article on the use of windows in the films of David Lynch for *Ciném'Action*.

CONTRIBUTORS

Angela K. Bayout is a writer living in San Francisco. As a child, her parents watched *Twin Peaks* when it first aired, and she would sneak out of bed to view it from a clandestine vantage point in the hallway. As an adult, she established and edited *Dionne's Story*, an anthology of poetry and prose inspired by the prevention of violence against women. Currently, she is the non-fiction editor of *The Written Wardrobe*, a fashion-inspired literary journal through ModCloth.com, where she is also a copywriter. Her poetry has appeared in *The Pittsburgh Post-Gazette* and the *Pittsburgh City Paper*, and you can find her personal essay in the forthcoming journal *Navigating the Heavens*. When she's not writing non-fiction or fiction on fairy tale, true crime, feminism or the paranormal, Angela is probably knitting and watching *Star Trek: The Next Generation*. You can follow her at www.angelakbayout.blogspot.com.

Kelly Bulkeley, Ph.D., is a visiting scholar at the Graduate Theological Union in Berkeley, California. He earned a doctorate in religion and psychological studies from the University of Chicago Divinity School, an M.T.S. from Harvard Divinity School, and a BA from Stanford University. A former president of the International Association for the Study of Dreams, and a senior editor of the APA journal *Dreaming*, he has written and edited several books on dream research. His recent works include *Dreaming in the World? Religions: A Comparative History* (New York University Press, 2008); *American Dreamers: What Dreams Tell Us about the Political Psychology of Conservatives, Liberals, and Everyone Else* (Beacon Press, 2008); and *Dreaming in the Classroom: Practices, Methods, and Resources in Dream Education* (SUNY Press, 2011). He is the director of the Sleep and Dream Database (SDDb), a digital archive and search engine designed to facilitate empirical dream research.

David Bushman is a television curator at The Paley Center for Media in New York, where he has organized a number of screening series over the past 20 years, including retrospective looks at presidential-campaign advertising, the programming of the Canadian Broadcasting Corporation, the television career of Steve Allen, and the evolution of the stand-up comedian on television. He previously was programming director at the cable channel TV Land, where he fought valiantly but futilely to bring *The Avengers* and *The Defenders* back to television, and a television editor at *Daily Variety* and *Variety*, and has taught and lectured on media at several colleges and other institutions. His particular area of expertise is television noir, and he is currently at work on a book on the subject.

Shara Lorea Clark is a *Peaks* fanatic and writer who was raised in the small town of Greenwood, Mississippi and currently resides in Memphis, Tennessee. She graduated summa cum laude with a degree in journalism from the University of Memphis. Her passion for writing blossomed in elementary school when she crafted her first poems about butterflies and love, and she now works for the *Memphis Flyer*, an alternative weekly newspaper. She is inspired by nature and intrigued by the mysteries of life and death. Her darker side loves horror films and craves answers to supernatural phenomena, which in part explains her fascination with the world of *Twin Peaks*. She is an adventurer, travelling as often as possible, in most cases to see live music by her favourite bands. Shara is a lover of hot black coffee, neatly stacked doughnuts and pie of all types, but has a penchant for cherry.

Dave Griffith is the author of *A Good War is Hard to Find: The Art of Violence in America* (Soft Skull Press, 2006). His essays and reviews have appeared in the *Utne Reader*, *The Normal School*, *IMAGE* and *Creative Nonfiction*, and online at Killing the Buddha. Currently, he is completing a manuscript titled *Pyramid Scheme: Making Art and Being*

Broke in America. He teaches creative writing at Sweet Briar College. He would like to thank his students in English 104 from the spring of 2012, and his research assistant, Monika Zaleska.

Gry Worre Hallberg is a scholar and performance artist operating at the interface of art and academia. She has, among others, performed with SIGNA and co-founded Fiction Pimps, Sisters Hope and Club de la Faye (a performance-oriented art collective operating in the space between fiction and reality). With her extensive background in research and practice of the performing arts and new economies, Gry is continuously investigating innovative ways to integrate the potential of an unfolded aesthetic dimension as an alternative to existing within the dominant system. This ultimately leads to a new paradigm, that she currently terms 'The Sensuous Society'. Her method is art-based research, and on several occasions, she has investigated the possibilities of new academic (re)presentation, including the project Unfolding Academia, a collaborative effort led by Goldsmiths' College in London, Freie Universität, Berlin, and the University of Copenhagen. Also see: gryworrehallberg.wordpress.com

Ulf Rathjen Kring Hansen holds a masters degree in modern culture and cultural communication from the University of Copenhagen. His thesis explored the emergence of hoax phenomena on the Internet. A man of many trades, he is also a radio producer, sound artist and journalist with a love for music, film and online culture. Also see: urkh. wordpress.com

Andrew Howe is an associate professor in the Department of History at La Sierra University where he teaches courses in American history, popular culture and film studies. Although a generalist by nature, with recent projects involving such widely disparate research subjects as the history of the hot dog and the FIFA World Cup as a means of negotiating political conflict, particular areas of interest include the science fiction genre, the films of Alfred Hitchcock and World War II. He is currently working on a book-length project focusing upon how biological invasions, extinctions and re-introductions are handled by the media. To that end, a recent sabbatical explored the manner in which the Africanized ('Killer') bee 'invasion' of the late 1970s/early 1980s was constructed as a threat by employing metaphors and terminologies culled from that era's debates about illegal immigration.

Joshua Minton is co-editor of The Red Room podcast and holds a BA in creative writing from Bowling Green State University. He continues to annoy friends and family with incessant references to Bob Dylan and *Battlestar Galactica*.

Chris Murray studied at NUI Dublin, Bristol and Warwick, and is currently a postdoctoral fellow in British-Asian Literature at Nanyang Technological University. His first book, *Tragic Coleridge* (Ashgate, 2013) argues that Samuel Taylor Coleridge's works manifest a philosophy of sacrifice drawn from Greek tragedy. His new project, *Romantics Reading China*, examines literary responses to Chinese culture. He is also writing about his experiences learning from a kung fu master in Singapore.

Fran Pheasant-Kelly is MA Award Leader and senior lecturer in film studies at the University of Wolverhampton, UK. Her research areas include abjection and space, which form the basis for her book, *Abject Spaces in American Cinema: Institutional Settings, Identity, and Psychoanalysis in Film* (I.B Tauris, 2013). Further research areas include fantasy and post-September 11 cinema, with publications including a forthcoming book, *Fantasy Film Post 9/11* (Palgrave Macmillan, 2013). Recent publications include 'Institutional Settings, Identity and Insanity: Abject Spaces in *Shutter Island*' in the *New Review of Film and Television* (Routledge, 2012); 'Authenticating the Reel: Realism, Simulation and Trauma in *United 93*' in V. Bragard, C. Dony and W. Rosenberg (eds), *Portraying 9/11: Essays on Representations of 9/11 in Comic Books, Literature, Film and Theatre* (McFarland Press, 2011); 'Ghosts of Ground Zero' in P. Hammond (ed.), *Screens of Terror* (2011); and 'The Ecstasy of Chaos: Mediations of 9/11, Terrorism and Traumatic Memory in *The Dark Knight*' in *Journal of War and Culture Studies* (2011).

Scott Ryan is co-editor of The Red Room podcast. He has run Superted Productions for 25 years, creating film, music and plays. He is currently directing his latest feature film, *Meet Abby*. He writes weekly entertainment articles at www.redroompodcast.com, and has been an avid *Twin Peaks* fan since it originally aired on television. Scott would really like Sheryl Lee to contact him for an interview: Feedback@redroompodcast.com

DIANE, 7:30 AM,
FEBRUARY TWENTY-FOURTH.
ENTERING TOWN OF TWIN PEAKS.
FIVE MILES SOUTH OF THE
CANADIAN BORDER, TWELVE MILES
WEST OF THE STATE LINE.
NEVER SEEN SO MANY TREES IN MY LIFE.
AS W.C. FIELDS WOULD SAY,
'I'D RATHER BE HERE THAN
PHILADELPHIA.'

DALE COOPER
SEASON 1, PILOT EPISODE